C0-ARQ-689

BURN a LITTLE!

(or, what's *LOVE* all about?)

By JOSEPH T. McGLOIN, S.J.

Illustrated by DON BAUMGART

THE BRUCE PUBLISHING COMPANY
MILWAUKEE

IMPRIMI POTEST:

Leo J. Burns, S.J.
Provincial, Wisconsin Province of the Society of Jesus

NIHIL OBSTAT:

John F. Murphy, S.T.D.
Censor librorum

IMPRIMATUR:

✠ William E. Cousins
Archbishop of Milwaukee
July 7, 1961

ACKNOWLEDGMENT

Grateful acknowledgment is made for the use of excerpts from a few of my articles in *The Queen's Work* and for permission to reproduce several of Don Baumgart's cartoons.

THE AUTHOR

Library of Congress Catalog Card Number: 61–17982

(2/62)

To
The Youth of The World

May Christ and Mary
always be the only Models
challenging enough
for them to imitate

INTRODUCTION

If you haven't read the first two books of this *Love — and Live!* series, maybe you'd better do so. They're called *Learn a Little!* and *Yearn a Little!*, and they contain some important background material leading up to this third and, for the moment, final book.

It's presumed here that, by now, you realize that there's a little more to life than a hamburger at the drive-in or a ham on TV — though these things have *some* importance, too. And this book will go into some really important, positive things in your life, pointing out to you just what your choice will be: the love of God (Burn a little!) or a completely selfish love of yourself. Actually, you'll either be a genuine saint or a real square. Take your choice.

But before anything else, let's take a good, honest look at *you*. This book would probably be a lot more popular if the entire introduction were taken up with *praising* youth, but youth prefers honesty to flattery, so let's be honest.

Communism today makes every effort to capture the souls of youth. And it's really a "capture," a *slavery* held out to them under the guise of "freedom."

But you know that well enough. You have no trouble at all recognizing the slavery that is Communism. You know perfectly well that Communism has no intention whatsoever of gaining freedom for men, only slavery.

Sure, you recognize the slavery of Communism readily enough — you've been trained to recognize it, despite the Communistic protestations of "freedom" and good will to men. And yet you are probably as enslaved right now as you'd ever be under Communism. You go around yelling about Communism and its enslavement, and you've voluntarily enslaved yourself just as thoroughly as any Communist dictator could enslave you forcibly. You have, in fact, often enough enslaved yourself to the very things Communism finds most praiseworthy — with no help from Khrushchev or any of the other loud little apostles of Communism.

But let's lay it right on the line. To say that you, youth, are a bunch of slaves requires some explanation.

Since the tragic day that Eve handed Adam an apple and he didn't have the courage to refuse to eat it, mankind has been enslaved as a group — enslaved to sin, to a *tendency* to sin. And not even your youth renders you immune from *that* sort of slavery — you are born into the world with it. But where the entire human race is enslaved by original sin, youth is enslaved today by more subtle things, inside you and outside you. You're enslaved by your passions, which say "Grab this moment of pleasure," and you're much too strongly shackled to say "No, I won't." In the realm of passions, you are probably most helplessly enslaved by self-centeredness, thinking primarily, secondarily, and finally of yourself. The outlook of youth *is* one of selfishness, because selfishness and immaturity go so well together. Your habitual primary consideration is not "What can I *contribute* to this, or to this person?" but rather "What's in it *for me?*" Be honest now for just a minute: How often, on retiring at night, when you examine your conscience and make an act of contrition — how often at that time can you say honestly that you have done a single, solitary thing that day which was done solely for someone else, out of charity and generosity, rather than for yourself?

So you're enslaved — by your own passions, and by your own self-seeking. And there are things outside you that play on these two things, that use them to enslave you even further. How many, for instance, will go against "custom," the things everyone seems to be doing? How many of you teen-aged girls are anything other than slaves to "fashion,"

It's really the loud-mouths we're afraid of — even though they are just a loud minority.

so much so that you wouldn't be caught dead being "unfashionable"? And how many of you — boys and girls alike — are so deathly afraid to go against that loudmouthed minority that sets itself up as "the crowd" that you'll even do things you suspect are wrong or that you *know* are wrong in order not to be thought a "square" — which is the term "the crowd" has for the right kind of nonconformist.

And how enslaved you are, too, to the advertisements, to the "images" you see all around you, so that the slavery that is Hollywood becomes your ideal — money, glamour, even a polite, polished, snobbish sort of sin.

You're so enslaved you fall for all these things. You suspect perhaps that "the crowd" is not really as big as it sounds, but it *is* loud and you're so enslaved by that very loudness that you fear its criticism. You suspect that "the crowd" is like the crazy man, who claims, as a defense mechanism, that everyone but himself is crazy, but you're *afraid* to do anything about it, because you're *slaves* to it. Maybe it's the other way round, that you're slaves *because* you're afraid, because you haven't the courage to become free. And, as far as following the crowd is concerned, this is all because of a group of loudmouths who are enslaved themselves and who seek, like the enslaved Satan, to shackle others as well. This is hell, you know — the eternal, desperate quest for fellow prisoners.

But we're talking about *you*. Why should you allow yourself to be enslaved by such an obvious crowd, which proposes slavery to you as freedom in such a way that you fall for it? I can almost see the protest on your faces. "We don't fall for it!" you'd like to insist. But, protest or not, and sad to say, you and I both know perfectly well that you do fall for it.

You have quite a few protests as a matter of fact, that get noised around in the newspapers and on TV panels you take part in and such. And, often enough, the protests are genuinely meant — in *theory*. Practice is another thing. Let's take a look at some of your favorites and see how you *act*, not how you *yell!*

Vocally and in print, you teen-agers have never been bashful in protesting that everything seemingly wrong with you as a group is not really your fault at all, but the fault of adults — your parents, your teachers, the adults who *lead* you. And there is, of course, a certain amount of truth in this. You don't write the filthy books or post the rotten pictures or produce the shows which are classified as "adult" only because they depict adultery.

All true. But what is false is that you seemingly think that these things would be produced even if there were no market for them. You do buy them. You do use them. And without your using them, they would long ago have ceased to exist. The teen-age market is certainly one of the biggest in the world, and no manufacturer, no printer, no producer is going to put things on that market if you refuse to buy them.

I'm not trying to excuse the adults, understand. But I'm not going to admit that you have no free will, either. You can take or leave what they offer. And if you'd leave it, it soon would not even be offered!

As a group, the group known in general as "youth" or "teen-agers," you go around shouting quite a number of meaningless clichés, among them such heart-rending appeals as "I want to be free," or "I want to be loved," or "I want to be treated as an individual and not as part of a mob."

And what does "freedom" connote to the ordinary teen-ager? It means slavery, because by his "freedom," the teen-ager wants to have the uninhibited use of things he is not prepared for: he wants to date excessively before nature ever intended him to date very much at all; he wants to "act" superficially as an adult without an adult's mental and emotional equipment; he wants unrestricted use of a car, even though this may be a weapon and an occasion of sin for him. These are the things he means by freedom, when in reality he's begging to be enslaved by all he asks for.

Youth yells aloud today that they want and need love — a fact it would be pretty hard to deny. And all the time, they haven't the foggiest notion of what the word even means. Teen-age magazines use a different word for it: "Why I flip for Frankie Avalon, or Fabian, or Tuesday Weld." I *flip for* somebody's long wavy polished hair or for some little girl's pathetic search for what she calls glamour. And is this the mature love the youth of today are screaming aloud for?

"Treat us as individuals" you shout in season and out of season — and there's nothing right-thinking adults would sooner do than treat you as individuals, nothing they would sooner see than your maturity and individuality coming to the fore, so that you are not dragged along by a crowd going the wrong way, so that you have the individuality and courage to act as an individual and not as part of a mob which is afraid of anything except the most abject conformity lest they be called "square." Oh yes, the magazines and papers which cater to youth are full of this appeal — to be considered a *person* — and the next thing that happens is that this same individuality-searching group is making a smash hit, breaking all records, out of a classic as individualistic as "Itsy Bitsy Teenie Weenie Yellow Polka Dot Bikini," sung by a highly individualistic representative of teen-age society with a highly individualistic duck-tail hairdo — like every other unmusical musical phenomenon that has made money off the individualistic teen-age music market of late. You want to be treated as a *person?* You want to be treated as *mature?* Do you want to be given responsibility? Then, I would say, if you want all these things, show first that you deserve them, that you *are* mature, that you *are* responsible, and that you *are* a person, one who is not carried along by the tide of popularity or whim or fashion or custom, or the fear of being called square by the loud mouths who constitute the crowd. Do this and you'll be treated as you wish — every time. Stick with the mob and you'll naturally be considered a part of it.

Ah, but *I* am different, you say. I am not a part of this mob. You object that I'm describing only the teen-ager of the headlines, of the sensational part of the press, and that you are not a part of the teen-agers of the headlines, that you are different. And it's devoutly to be hoped that you're correct, that you are not a part of this particular mob, that you *are* different. So let's admit you're not just a part of a mob, that you have individuality, that you can be a non-conformist when that is necessary.

But if this is true, what are you *doing* about the teen-agers of the headlines? If you're not a part of *that* mob, then you must be a part of a silent crowd that shows by its silence that it agrees with everything in the headlines? Why, if you're not a part of the immature, conforming, helplessly slavish crowd that sets teen-age fashion and thereby gains the right to loudly call everyone else a "square," why are *you* so silent? Why, if you aren't the teen-agers of the headlines, aren't you making some headlines of your own? Why must the enslaved teen-ager be the only one who is publicized, when you, who boast of being free, are never heard from? Why can't there be headlines about your maturity, your responsibility, your charity and unselfishness toward the rest of the human race? Why can't there be headlines about the number of teens at daily Communion instead of the sneering jibes about teens at drive-ins and in drag races in the streets? Why must we hear and read, most of the time, only about the stupid, childish and fake, pathetic efforts at seeming maturity made by the teen-ager of the headlines? If you don't like the teen-ager of the headlines, where are *your* headlines?

That's the negative side of the picture. Let's not give excuses for ourselves or for other teens. Let's face them and ourselves and see what we're going to do about it. Above all, let's be honest. Let's not call ourselves free when we're really slaves. Let's not mistake slavery for freedom, just because some loudmouthed juvenile delinquent who makes his living off your weaknesses tells you it's so. Let's turn to the positive side of the question, and see just what real freedom is.

And the definition of real freedom is simple, so simple it makes the complicated snares of slavery seem ridiculous. You have to judge real freedom by your real purpose in life: Anything which helps you to fulfill that purpose is freedom;

anything which keeps you from it is slavery. You have one purpose, and one only. There is no purpose for you outside of saving your soul, getting to God in heaven for all eternity. Miss that purpose, and you might as well never have lived, because your life in that case would be an utter, complete, 100 per cent flop. You fulfill that purpose by means equally simple, by knowing, loving, and serving God in this life. Again, simple. And you know, love, and serve God, by using the things He put on this earth for you to use, *for that purpose and for that alone*. The conclusion from that is simple, too: you must use the things around you — your own talents, your boy and girl friends, the literature and entertainment around you — to get to know, love, and serve God and so return to Him for all eternity. And until you can do that you are a slave. You are not free. You are not mature, nor worthy of the name of person nor of responsibility, nor of any of the things you crave so badly, or at least so loudly.

This, then, is real freedom — the freedom to know, love, and serve God — and anything else, anything that keeps us from this purpose, is complete and utter, even if pitiable, slavery.

Freedom is following Christ nailed to a cross. You, too, paradoxically enough, have to be nailed to the cross with Him before you are really free. And you'll never achieve that sort of freedom through slavish conformity to a mob that might otherwise call you a "square."

And yet you have all the hope and all the chances of success in the world. You, of all people, have the opportunity to be really free, with what Christ called "the freedom of the sons of God." You have so much to work with to achieve that purpose that it's going to be sheer tragedy if you don't use all you have.

Your potentialities, your abilities are enormous. The power you have of physical, intellectual, and spiritual accomplishment is almost unlimited, *if* you use that ability. Remember

Actually, you have company on the road to goodness, and it's the noisy propagandist for evil who's really alone.

the parable Christ told of the three people who were given certain talents to work with? One was given ten, another five, and a third one talent. The eager beaver who was given ten talents put them to work and gained ten more. And the one with five gained five more with his. But the knucklehead with one talent went out and buried it! He displayed this talent to his master, proud as a giddy puppy that he hadn't lost it, even though he had done nothing with it, proud as you may be some day when you hand over your intellect, your physical and spiritual capabilities to Christ with the stupid boast that you "at least didn't lose them." And undoubtedly in such a case you'll be called the same name as this one-talent genius, "an unprofitable servant."

You have these things. *Use* them for the purpose God intended — to get back to Him.

You young people have high ideals, higher, perhaps, in some cases than those of your elders. But don't let them remain only ideals — put them into practice instead of daydreaming your life away on frothy and merely theoretical ideals.

You have great courage — the courage to do what's right, the courage to be fair to people of all races and religions, to beautiful people or ugly, the courage to be *free*. Use that courage to speak out for what you know is right in the face of the stupid crowd, and to *do* what you know is right no matter what the oddballs who might loudly call you a square might think.

You have energy to burn. Don't burn it on a slag heap, or a garbage dump. Burn it in the knowledge, love, and service of Christ, in the salvation of yourself and your neighbor, in your own sanctification — the only things that will really make you free and that really count. What a horrible thing if you come to that moment when all your youthful energy is gone, burned out, and you've wasted it on trifles.

And you have another asset which you all too often forget — deafened, perhaps, by the loud mouths who constitute "the crowd." You have companions on this road you travel. They're not the loud mouths, not the big spenders nor the frauds who make money and gain fame from your weaknesses. They're the quiet, calm, mature young people who are trying their best to do what God wants, without fanfare and without headlines. And they're the vast majority of teen-agers. Because the vast majority of youth is *free,* though their publicity isn't gaudy.

Be free, too, to read this book and ponder its rather serious thoughts. And, right now, be prepared to *face* thoughts which are serious, sometimes unpleasant, and even, on occasion, humanly speaking, frightening.

CONTENTS

chapter I

LAST THINGS FIRST

There are people who always try to avoid thinking of unpleasant subjects, even when these subjects *must* be faced. One of our entertainers (the kind who can never entertain himself) used to bawl out anyone who mentioned the word "death" or "morgue" in his presence. This is not only *avoiding* reality — it's using it as a steppingstone to mental illness.

Scarlett O'Hara of *Gone With the Wind* fame had a better, yet somewhat similar, type of philosophy. When any unpleasant subject entered Scarlett's rather sharp little mind, she would simply tell herself, "I won't think of that now. I'll think of it tomorrow." Now this is not a bad philosophy on occasion, but there are times, too, when we can no longer postpone issues but will have to face them.

Among the countless things which keep psychiatrists in business is the reluctance many people have to face reality. And it wouldn't be a very risky bet that among the unrealistic dreamers of the world, teen-agers are pretty well represented.

Dreaming can be a good thing, you know, when it's combined with a good square look at reality. In fact, the great things which have become reality have always been the achievements of dreamers of a sort. But *unrealistic* dreaming is just a waste of time, an excuse for laziness. So, let's dream our dreams, but at the same time, let's not shut our eyes to reality. Let's not dream of making square circles or sticks with one end; let's dream of doing the great things which are worthwhile *and* possible.

At the top of the voting list of "things we'd prefer to forget" is one little item that stands all by itself — and that's the thought of death. But if it's true that we'd sooner think of anything except our own death, it's also true that there is no more inevitable reality for any of us. And you simply can't have any realistic outlook on life unless you're willing, strangely enough, to face the fact of death. So let's be realistic for a short spurt. Let's not shut our eyes and whistle as we go by the corner where death lurks. Let's stop and take a good look at this mysterious character, whether he turns out to be friend or enemy. After all — to be realistic — we have to make his acquaintance sooner or later anyhow. You can't avoid *that* little bit of realism. And if you wait until you *have* to meet death, you may learn a lot about it but you're not going to teach anybody about it.

Now whenever someone starts to talk about death, our tendency is to look on him as a creep of some sort, as a guy who's a little on the morbid side. And it is true that you don't become the life of the old party by smiling cheerfully at the guys and gals as you start a conversation on death. It just isn't a subject that goes well with the ordinary smile, and you have to be pretty careful of any extraordinary smiles you flash around, too, while you talk about this subject. I once made a retreat under an otherwise expert retreat master who smiled cheerfully, if forcedly, as he introduced the meditation on death. "Tomorrow," he said, "let's consider death. Let us begin by imagining ourselves in our coffins." This turned out to be quite a meditation. The combination of a somewhat ghoulish smile and a coffin was just too much for any meditation to withstand.

But, in actual fact, the consideration of death, while naturally serious, is not in itself morbid unless *we* make it so. After all, if we are not completely fooled by the fake worldly propaganda all around us (which tells us that if we don't look at death, it will go away), we must realize that death is really a *good* thing. It is mysterious, true, and therefore frightening. Not too many people come back to tell us what death is like. And God never intended us to lose this fear entirely. We are supposed to *work* our way to heaven, to counter real uncertainties with faith and trust in God. And you don't find a better little prompter to faith and trust than death.

Figure it out — if you had a perfectly clear picture of the heaven that is going to be yours after death, you would have no fear of the mystery of death and no need for blind faith and trust in God. Death would be no trial. And this would be quite a contradiction, since death is supposed to be one of the big ones, the final exam on our way to God. Only through faith and trust in God are we going to dispel our natural fear of death and pass through it as we should — in anticipation of the unimaginable joy that will be ours forever with God. This is the way it's supposed to be. We are made for eternal happiness with God and for nothing else. But the only way we can get to God is through death. So death is bad? Come on — think with your mind and not your emotions. It isn't when you *face* death that it's terrifying — it's when you *refuse* to face it.

The one sure thing about death is that there's no escaping it for any of us. Every now and then some crackpot shows up who has a plan to keep from dying, and we just nod patiently and wait, knowing that sooner or later he and his theory will both be dead. Another obvious fact going with the inevitability of death is that it is sort of permanent. No dress rehearsals, no nothing. Not only can't you take it with you — you can't come back and get it either!

So there really isn't much use in asking yourself if you're *going* to die. Let's try another question for size: *When* are you going to die? Now *there's* an interesting question if ever there was one. If only you knew its definite answer!

The old bromide that you can't promise yourself another hour happens to be perfectly true. In fact, it's an understatement. You can't even promise yourself another minute. If it's God's will that you die at this very moment, good-by. You'll never finish reading this book.

It would be exceedingly simple for God to allow you to die right now. All He'd have to do, for instance, is allow your heart to stop. One of your arteries could clog up for a few minutes, and that would be it. Or your breath could stop operating. After all, God keeps these things going. He can allow them to stop just as easily. You live or die by God's will, and even your apparent health doesn't have much to do with it.

You and I, no matter how young or how old we are, no matter how healthy or sick, are dying at this very moment. We've really been dying since we were born, because we get closer to death at every moment. Let's not kid ourselves. Your life is shorter now that it was when you picked up this book. And *that's* a process you can't do anything about.

So we know that we could die at any time, and that we inevitably come closer to death at every moment. Christ summed up the situation about as well as possible when He said death would come "like a thief in the night." No thief gives much warning, and this thief will be no exception.

Some years ago, in a national magazine, there was a picture of a beautiful young girl, about twenty years old, going up the front steps of a church to her wedding. The next picture showed her collapsed on those same steps, dead, without warning and with no hint that death could be near. It came "like a thief in the night."

Often, as we grow older, we see our contemporaries and others dying around us. Sometimes they have some warning. Just as frequently, they do not. They do not follow seniority either, but seem to die at any age and in almost any state of health. They go by accident, by sickness, or they just go. Yes, even teen-agers die sometimes. Sorry, but there's no guarantee that you are going to get out of your teens alive.

I don't know what the statistics are for the whole country, but I do know that in one high school in which I taught, death too enrolled occasionally. In most classes there had been at least one student who died either before or very shortly after graduation. A few years ago, five of our boys died in a single school term, three in accidents, one from cancer, and one from leukemia. One was a senior, two were juniors, and two were sophomores. The year before we had lost a freshman. Death doesn't even care what class you're in or when graduation is.

You can't guarantee, in other words, that you'll be around next year reading any books. You can't guarantee that you'll be here tomorrow, and as a matter of fact, as times goes on, the odds lessen. It might be a 100–1 chance that you'll be here tomorrow, but by the next day the odds are down, and one of these days they'll be about 50–50. And from that point on, the odds start going into reverse.

So far we don't have very enlightening answers to our questions. *Am* I going to die? Of course. Not a doubt in the world. *When* am I going to die? When God so wills it. Only God can make it more definite than that.

But if we can't do anything about the fact or about the date, we do have some influence on the answer to the next question: *How?* Now by this question, I don't mean here the means or anything like that, but rather the *condition* we'll be in spiritually when we die. Will we be in the state of grace or in the state of mortal sin at that moment? Another way of putting the question would be to ask if we're going to heaven or hell.

Will you die right after you have committed a mortal sin? Or will you die, perhaps, in the very act of committing a mortal sin? Will you die without a chance to get to confession, or even before you can make an act of perfect contrition? These are good questions, questions we should ask ourselves before we sin, *long* before we sin, right now, as a matter of fact. You see, the answer to this question of how we're going to die is pretty simple: *We are probably going to die exactly as we live*. And we're kidding ourselves, taking an awful chance that we'll die in the state of grace if we live in the state of mortal sin. The odds against *that* are too great to risk.

One of our most famous millionaires, who had more millions than he or his descendants could possibly use, spent the last moments on his deathbed trying to make even more millions. He was dictating letters, trying to figure ways and means of making more money, even as he breathed his last. And, of course, not even one dollar of his vast wealth went with him. He couldn't even appreciate his expensive casket.

The Nazis of Hitler's Germany had dedicated their lives so completely to *Der Führer* that they could not turn their thoughts elsewhere even at death. And as they lived for Hitler, for Hitler they also died. We don't change at death. If we live for God's creatures, neglecting Him, we won't turn to Him on our deathbed. We'll try to stick with the creatures we've devoted our lives to.

It's the same way with grace and sin. You aren't going to change the habits of a lifetime just because you happen to be dying. Oh, there are such things as deathbed conversions — shoestring catches if you will. But don't ever count on it, because apparently there are more errors than catches. Occasionally you encounter people who have turned away from God and stayed that way for years, sometimes with the idea that they'll come back on their deathbeds. Then, when their time comes to die, they'll start to argue that God doesn't want them back now. In other words, the state of despair can follow more closely and unexpectedly than anyone can predict.

There was once a young priest who went to a certain house to try to bring back a man who had spent much of his life away from God. The priest tried his best to argue this charac-

Probably no one cares to be stared at, especially when he's dying.

ter into turning back to God so that he'd be eligible for an eternity with Him rather than an eternity in hell. But the priest didn't get anywhere at all, as the old man parried every argument with some foolish reply or other. When the priest told him that he was going to suffer for all eternity, the old boy would just shake his head sadly and say he deserved it (Not that there's any arguing about this — we all *deserve* it!), and he'd go on to say that he'd hurt God so much that God wouldn't want him back now — goofy "arguments" like that.

Finally, after the priest had tried every argument he knew, with no luck, he shrugged, grabbed a chair, and sat in a corner of the room staring at the man on the bed. Now no one likes to be stared at — particularly, I presume, if he's dying and he's not 100 per cent optimistic about his future. So, finally, our dying friend blew his stack and shouted at the priest, "How come you're staring at me that way? Get out of here!"

The priest just smiled and went on staring.

Finally, the old boy began to shout and rave. "What's the big idea?" he yelled. "Why don't you get out? You're not going to convert me."

"That's right, I guess," the priest answered cheerfully. "But, you see, I haven't been ordained very long. I've only seen a few people die, and as far as I know, I've never actually watched a person go to hell. If you don't mind, I'd like to sit here and watch you do it." That did it. The old man finally woke up before he went out for good.

I haven't been able to track down the priest in this story, but, true or not, the story has a point. Unfortunately, not too many such stories have happy endings.

So that's a little food for thought on the "how" of our dying. But maybe we should have considered, briefly at least, just what dying is. Let's do that now. We can best do it, perhaps, by checking the differences between life and death. And, in doing this, inevitably we'll have to think a little bit about our own possible death.

What's the difference between life and death? Well, there are a few rather obvious differences to start with. Lift your arm, for instance, and look at your hand, something you've always taken for granted. And yet it's a pretty complicated mechanism. You can move the fingers. You know that your blood is pumping through that hand with pretty fair regularity. It goes quite a distance to get there, too — through your whole body. Probably, too, you're doing some breathing at the moment — another pretty remarkable process you simply take for granted. Everything, in fact, is going along pretty much according to custom. No particular hitches.

But some day, sooner or later, you aren't going to be able to lift your arm or bend your fingers or turn your head or even take a breath. All these things that you take for granted now are suddenly going to be out of order. Not that this will matter to you then, because a really important part of you is gone. Your soul has taken off for another climate, cool or overheated, as the case may be.

As far as your body is concerned, however, someone else will move your hands around, putting them in a nice pious position on your chest with a Rosary wrapped around them. Someone will undoubtedly try his best to make you look decent so that your relatives can look at you in your casket and remark on how nice you look. You've seen corpses? Well, this time you're the corpse. That's death — no breath, no blood circulating, and your soul and body separated. *You* have moved out. And you'll never move back. The body you took such good care of is only good now for helping to push up a few daisies.

Not the most pleasant thoughts, these, but they have to be faced anyhow. The first conclusion you arrive at when you think of death this way is that your body alone really isn't worth wasting a lifetime on, and if you spend your whole life looking only for bodily comfort and pleasure, all you've done is waste a life. Of course, a good, reasonable amount of care ought to be given to your body — its health and presentableness and so on — because it's part of *you*. But there's no use giving *exclusive* attention to something that isn't going to last anyhow.

Death must be a time of very great loneliness, because this is one trip we'll have to make alone. When we were

No matter how old we get, we'll always be like lonely kids in the face of death.

kids, we were usually scared to go anywhere without an adult or two along — our parents, for instance. And the reason for this was that *everything* is a mystery to us in childhood, and we're afraid to venture into the unknown without a strong guiding hand. No matter how old we get, we're always going to be kids in the face of death, because nobody ever solves this mystery and survives. But, badly as we'll want company on this trip, we can't have any. No parents, no boy or girl friends, no police escorts. It has to be a solo.

And since you can't take anything or anybody with you, it's silly to dedicate your whole life to any creature. Imagine how a man must feel at death if he's dedicated his entire life to amassing wealth. And imagine the sense of loss you're going to feel at the time of death if you've spent all your time and energy on one of God's creatures, a boy or a girl perhaps, instead of God. In that case you'll be leaving friends when you die and going to a stranger. All your friends can do for you is cry and pray a little. And, all too soon, they'll probably forget you.

Think about these things for a while. Again, let's not be morbid about it, but realistic. Take a look at the fact of death, occasionally and calmly. Realize that inevitably it will come to you — this is your destiny as a human being. But realize, too, that it is only mysterious and not frightening. And above all, put your trust in God. All that separates you from Him and perfect happiness is this mysterious thing we know as death.

But you can't look at death all by itself and get anywhere. You have to look forward to the things that follow death as well.

And the thing that is going to follow right on the heels of death is our judgment. Immediately after we die, with no time to think things over, much less to *start* over, we are going to stand before Christ and be judged. And in that moment we are going to be sentenced to either heaven or hell for all eternity. (Of course, there *is* purgatory, unless the end of the world should happen to come about that time. In fact, that wouldn't be a bad time to go, if — .) We might wish, at the moment of judgment, that things had been different, but everything will be past tense then with regard to meriting or changing our minds. There is no future then but eternity, and any decisions will then be out of our hands. We will have made our decisions, time after time, through a lifetime before this. And all that judgment consists in is Christ's locating us according to our own previous choice — heaven or hell.

You see, immediately after your death, there is only going

to be one question of importance, and that is: "How did you live?" The question, "How do you *wish* you had lived?" is really useless at the time of death because such a wish can never be anything but a *wish* after death. You are going to be recognized by Christ either as one of His friends or as a stranger who neglected Him for a lifetime. If He's a stranger to you, you may find His eyes very cold and a little sad as He says to you, "Depart, ye cursed, into everlasting fire. . . ." If, on the other hand, He's been your friend, His smile will welcome you as He tells you to "Come, ye blessed of my Father, and enter the kingdom prepared for you. . . ." And, once said, neither set of words can be revoked. That will be that.

Now it is consoling to think of heaven and how wonderful it will be, infinitely surpassing any happiness we could know or even imagine on earth. Not so pleasant is the thought of hell, but it's one of those things that, pleasant or not, you sometimes have to think about. And maybe if you think about it a little, you'll never see it. In other words, you don't exactly try to scare the hell out of yourself, but rather scare yourself out of hell.

There was once a man who had the habit of smoking in bed. Not only that, but he also had the habit of falling asleep when he smoked. The first time this happened, he succeeded in burning up a part of his room. He himself was lucky enough to escape without injury. He was warned, of course, by the fire department, which takes a dim view indeed of people who fall asleep smoking in bed. But this character's stupidity was chronic, and so the same thing happened again. This time he wasn't so lucky, and he came up with a few burns. Well, he tried it a third time, and — you guessed it — this time he was cured. He was also burned to death.

You can tell some people time and time again that smoking in bed is extremely dangerous, and they'll never believe you until it's too late.

You can warn them about smoking in bed right up to their cremation.

In a sense, you're getting a warning right now. Reading a book, even one like this, is a form of God's grace. In God's Providence you did pick up this book, so it could be that God expects you to get something out of it. At the moment maybe you can pick up a good, healthy fear of hell. So read on.

Since you're being given the grace *now* of thinking about this horrible place called hell, your reaction should be one of gratitude rather than fear. There's still time to avoid the place, so thank God for this chance. After all, chances are that you could be in hell right at this moment instead of sitting around rather comfortably and reading about it. If you've ever committed a mortal sin, you could have died right after it. (You could do a lot worse than getting on your knees for a few seconds right now to thank God for this and the other favors He's done for you — for instance, for the tremendous amount of grace He's often given you to keep you out of sin.)

Only the fool, of course, is not afraid of the things that call for fear. To drive a car recklessly, with no fear, is stupid. To hitch a ride on an Atlas missile would show a lot more foolishness than bravery. Courage is the *overcoming* of fear, and not the absence of fear. So let's not be moronic about hell and not fear it. Let's be so afraid of it that we make very sure we never go there.

Hell is a *reality*. It's not something someone dreamed up or imagined. And so we're not facing all of reality if we refuse to face the fact of hell. We're just making like an ostrich that way. After all, it's possible that even some readers of this book *could* go to hell. Too bad, but true.

Christ seemed to want to make certain that the fact of hell should become very real to us. Now Christ was certainly the kindest, most gentle of people. And yet this kindly, gentle Christ, this Christ who cured the sick and forgave the greatest sinners, mentions the existence of hell or describes it some 70 or 80 times in the New Testament! This fact alone should make you do some serious thinking and praying. If our loving Christ mentioned so often something as gruesome as hell, He must have done it to try to keep us out of there. This would seem to make some sense, no?

You know, it's a great and wonderful privilege to be a Catholic — a tremendous gift of God, as a matter of fact. But I sometimes wonder if some of us Catholics don't sometimes start to believe that we *deserve* such a gift. At least I have seen some Catholics who seemed to look down on those of other faiths — as though they themselves could have the *gift* of faith by their own doing. Similarly, I'm afraid that occasionally you encounter an attitude on the part of some Catholics which seems to hold the rather consoling, but also rather stupid opinion that no Catholic can go to hell.

Sorry, but, Catholic or not, you don't get to heaven automatically. You still have to do it with the combination of God's grace and your own will. And just as the non-Catholic in good faith and the state of grace can get to heaven, so the Catholic can die in the state of mortal sin and lose his soul. We can't judge the spiritual condition of any person, but you probably won't have to look too far to spot a Catholic who seems to be in danger of going to hell for all eternity, someone who is not co-operating with God's grace and who is not living according to his Catholic principles. An unpleasant subject, this, so let's just say a little prayer for such people here and now and go on.

It would also seem to make some sense to suppose that if you or any other Catholic should end up in hell, you would probably be buried more deeply there than some of the others. Now that may seem a startling statement, but, startling or not, it's probably true. You have, after all, been given many more helps to get to heaven than have others. You have, for instance, such tremendous sacraments as penance, in which your sins can be forgiven at any time, and the sacrament of the Holy Eucharist, in which you can actually receive Christ Himself! If you and I can't avoid hell with helps such as these, then it looks like we'd rate a pretty deep spot there.

St. Francis of Assisi was supposed to have had a vision of hell once, and, when questioned as to whether he had seen any Franciscans there, had replied that he had not. This answer seemed to cause some surprise in his questioner, and so he asked, "How come?" St. Francis merely told him, "You have to look very deep in hell to see a Franciscan." I'm sure St. Francis didn't look on the members of his order as greater sinners than others, but he did realize that they had been given so many graces that if they flubbed it, they would deserve the worst punishments. And it's that way with *all* Catholics — God has lavished His gifts upon us.

It may be one neglected grace that will cause you, a Catholic, to go to hell. Certainly one neglected fault can grow until it puts you there. It may be one bad habit that you didn't conquer, although you had God's help if you had chosen to use it. Maybe you'll refuse to break with the one bad companion who will lead you to hell, someone you consider more important at the time than co-operating with God's grace. Maybe you'll neglect the grace of one retreat. Maybe you'll read all this about hell, and realize its importance, but will tell yourself, like Scarlett O'Hara, "I'll think of that tomorrow." Any one of these things could cause you trouble.

But keep in mind, too, that there is someone who can keep you out of hell. God can't keep you out of there — blasphemous as that statement might sound. No, there is only one person who can keep you from hell — with God's help, of course — and that person is *you.* Only you can make the decision to co-operate with God's grace and so go to heaven, to eternal happiness. Only you can decide whether you're going to serve God or turn away from Him.

Let's try to get a good close look at hell to see what it's like. We know a little bit about hell by the very way we sometimes use the word. When we say we had "a hell of a time," we usually mean something extremely unpleasant. You could multiply such examples, but there's no use. You get the point. Hell *is* something unpleasant, something we don't like, something horrible. Hell is really hell. Christ made it more definite when He told us that hell is fire, never ending, never consuming fire.

Probably, in the realm of suffering, there is nothing that can inspire more dread than fire. Talk to any fireman about the horrible things he has experienced and seen on his job, and you'll get some idea of the terrible suffering fire can cause. Recall some of the news pictures of hotel fires, where people would jump out the windows to their death rather than face the flames. Talk to the men who flew our bombers in World War II and in Korea, and they'll tell you that the thing they feared most wasn't death, but fire. Think back to

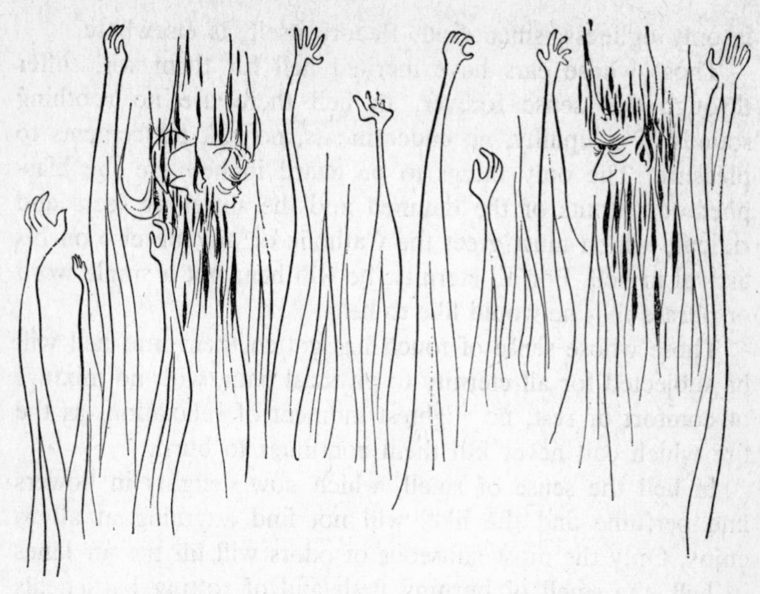

Hell is never-ending, never-consuming fire.

some of the news stories you've seen — of men trapped in burning trucks or cars. Recall the stories of Pearl Harbor and Hiroshima. Look at the pictures and watch men fighting with flame throwers. What reaction do you get from all this horror? If you're thinking at all, you should come up with a good, healthy fear of fire, and therefore a real fear of hell.

But the fire is only part of it. Since hell is *complete* suffering, and contains *no* pleasure or happiness, then it must be true that, just as the person who gets to heaven is going to find perfect joy and pleasure, so the poor guy who ends up in hell will find only complete pain, of both body and soul. And so, if we could pay a short visit to hell, we'd see people suffering eternally through every one of their senses. People who used their eyes to get themselves into hell will find those eyes forever tortured. Their eyes will rest on nothing pleasant or pleasurable here, nothing beautiful. Because in hell there is only ugliness, since God, Beauty itself, is elsewhere.

Those whose ears have merited hell for them will suffer through this sense forever. In hell there are no soothing sounds of sympathy, no endearments, no soft enticements to pleasure. The only things to be heard in hell are the blasphemous shouts of the damned and the shrieking jeers and ridicule which must greet the Catholic or anyone else on his arrival in hell. For all eternity, he will hear not a single word or phrase that he would like to hear.

Those whose sense of touch has gotten them into hell will be subjected for all eternity to physical pain, with no mixture of comfort or rest, no slightest moment of relaxation, as the fire which can never kill them continues to burn.

In hell the sense of smell, which now delights in flowers and perfume and the like, will not find anything at all to enjoy. Only the most nauseous of odors will fill the air lanes in hell, the smell of burning flesh and of rotting battlefields and of massive garbage pits — the revolting odor of sin, which has no perfume connected with it.

Closely allied with our sense of smell is that of taste, and this sense, too, will have its own peculiar tortures in hell. The gluttons who end up in hell are going to feel only eternal hunger and thirst, the pain of those in a lifeboat without food or water. Only now will they realize what a stupid bargain they made — a momentary, forbidden satisfaction of their taste for an eternity of frustration. There aren't many kinds of suffering comparable to thirst, but this is only one of the varieties hell has to offer.

Maybe you've sometimes figured that if you ever end up in hell you'll at least have some company. And this has a certain amount of truth to it at that. But it's certainly not going to be the sort of company you'd grow endeared to. In this world, there are some pretty low type characters in places like the prisons for the violently and criminally insane. But you would probably find that these people in the worst of the maximum security prisons are really rather nice folks, sort of homey, lovable people, compared with those you see in hell.

Or maybe it will occur to you that some of your present companions, including some pretty attractive guys and gals, might be there too. But just remember this — there is no beauty, no love, no companionship in hell, but only eternal hatred and loneliness. And think how deeply you will hate and be hated by someone who helped you to get there! You will have to face such a person for all eternity, and to realize at every moment the ugliness you traded for God, who is eternal Beauty. In heaven there would have been God and *His* people — the peaceful, the eternally happy, the souls who are enjoying the possession of God and of perfect happiness for all eternity. Their joy and peace and goodness would be obvious. But those in hell can have no joy, no peace, no calmness. Theirs is an eternal restlessness and dissatisfaction.

It's probably hard for us to realize, surrounded as we are by materialism and all the supercomforts of our modern civilization, but the fact is that we can suffer more through our higher faculties than we can through the lower faculties, such as our senses. Just as our happiness can be greater when it's on an intellectual or spiritual level, so our suffering can be essentially greater on this level also. And so we have to realize, although it might be hard to do so, that the greatest suffering in hell is going to come through our intellect and will.

If you manage to get to hell, it's not going to be only because of your body or senses, but it will be because you didn't use your God-given intellect or free will properly — to choose God instead of hell. There is no one in hell who did not *know* that what he did was wrong and did not *choose* to be there.

I suppose that one of the things that will torture our intellect most in hell is the realization that our whole and entire

After death, there are no "Round Trip" tickets to hell.

purpose in life — eternal happiness with God — is now frustrated, completely and eternally. Going with that will be the equally unpleasant knowledge that we could have done better, that we could have avoided hell rather easily and that now there is no chance whatsoever of changing our minds. This sense of complete loss and complete frustration, the never ending, irreparable loss of everything we were born for, must be *the* pain of hell — no happiness, no love, no joy forever.

And that little word *forever* is going to cause us quite a

little trouble in hell, too. The realization that there is no going back and starting over for us, no chance in our future for anything but pain and frustration, must be the grimmest of eternity's punishments. Because hell is like a clock with only one hand, which shows the minutes but never advances an hour. There are no hours in hell. Time after time after time, the big hand on the clock goes around and each time it reaches sixty, all it does is start over again.

Christ gave us a pretty good summary of what hell is like in the simple little story of Dives and Lazarus. Lazarus, you will remember, was the poor beggar who used to lie outside Dives's door and beg for bread. And Dives couldn't be bothered. Then, as Christ tells the story, both men died, with Lazarus ending up in heaven and Dives in hell. And we are told that Dives shouted up to Lazarus and begged him to dip his hand in some water and bring just one drop for his tongue, because, as he said, "I am consumed in this flame." And we're told that Lazarus had to refuse — regretfully. This is a picture of hell. No way out. No letup of suffering — ever.

So that's a little look at hell. But what can you say about heaven? Not very much, really, especially when even St. Paul has to say that eye has not seen nor ear heard what God has prepared for us there. (And, after all, if we *could* see heaven, this life would no longer be a trial.) We know it's the opposite of hell in all respects — sharing eternal goodness instead of associating with never ending evil; unmitigated joy instead of pain and suffering; eternal love instead of eternal hatred. And, above all, heaven is the possession of God — all loveliness, lovableness, and happiness, our destiny. That's heaven. Let's make sure we see it at firsthand some day.

Those are called "the four last things" — death, judgment, heaven, and hell. And never was a word used so accurately. They really *are* last. Don't look for another chance after you run into these things.

chapter II

THE "HAPPY FALL" OF ADAM

I suppose we lost a few readers on that last chapter, because it wasn't the most cheerful little thing in the world, and there are always those who refuse to face reality. But if you're still around, cheer up — that's the end of that sort of thing for now, and we can go on to something a lot more cheerful, a lot more interesting, and, undoubtedly, a lot more important. Just remember that we considered these things — death, judgment, heaven, and hell — to give ourselves a true sense of values. Now let's look at some really enormous values. And to do that, we have to look back in history a way.

Adam and Eve, when they sinned, really fouled things up. They had a pretty good chance of keeping the whole human race on a relatively easy path forever. But they flubbed it. Let's take a quick look at these first parents of ours. We know that they were born in a state called "original justice." And in that state they were the possessors of very exceptional gifts: They had the tremendous supernatural gift of sanctifying grace, the friendship of God. They were the temples of the Holy Spirit. They had a gift called integrity, which meant that, unlike us, they could *control* their senses and themselves with their intellect and will much more easily than we can. They were to be free from death and sickness and pain — little things like that. You might say they had it made.

But you might be wrong, too, because, despite great gifts like this, they did manage to sin.

I can almost hear you saying, as almost everyone else has,

"What a couple of stupes! Why, if I had been in their shoes — that is, their place . . ." Not so fast, friend. Judging from our own past performances, most of us probably wouldn't have done any better than Adam and Eve. As a matter of fact, while the gifts they had were pretty terrific, we have at least one gift right now that puts even integrity into its shadow — Christ in the Holy Eucharist.

So let's not be too rough on our first parents. We have nothing to brag about either.

Now when Adam and Eve failed their test, that could have ended things right there as far as the human race was concerned. (Just as one sin could end it for *us*.) But an almost unbelievable phenomenon took place in history. Adam and Eve sinned, and in so doing committed a terrible offense against God, who had created them. And this same God, instead of looking at their ingratitude, looked on them with love and said, "I will send my Son to redeem them." Not only is there no other example of mercy like this throughout the pages of history, but there couldn't possibly be. Let's take a quick look at this phenomenon called the Redemption.

Keep in mind that this is a man who has sinned, a tiny creature, but one capable of offering this insult to God, his Creator. And so, if a man has sinned, and if there is going to be any redemption, somehow it must be a man who tries to make up for sin.

Another fact we'll have to keep in mind is that the seriousness of an offense is judged not just by the status of the offender, but also by the one offended. You won't have any trouble seeing the truth of that statement if you look at a few examples.

Suppose you see an ant and step on it. Now, without any reason for it, that isn't the worst action in the world. It isn't really good either. No unreasonable action is. Or suppose you go down the street and kick a dog. Now that's a little different. Dogs are not supposed to be kicked. So it seems a

You just can't admire people who make a practice of kicking dogs around.

little worse to kick a dog than it does to step on an ant. (Me—I like dogs better than ants. And they seem to like me better.) Or suppose you kick a few people around, one of your companions, say. Now this could be a little worse than kicking a dog. (This could be argued, with some real sly remarks pro and con, but I think you get the point.) Or suppose that you go and hit your pastor. There may have been people who wanted to push their pastor around on occasion, but after all he does hold a place of dignity; so it's a rather great offense to give in to the impulse. But suppose you sneak past a few security guards and kick the President of the United States. Or you make a pilgrimage to Rome and take a poke at the Pope. By this time you're tired, and so are lots of other people. The point of all this should be obvious — the offense gets greater in proportion to the dignity of the one offended. In the examples just given, *you* remain the same lovable person you always were, but the offense gets progressively greater as your targets change.

Now, apply this principle to sin. Adam, a man, had sinned.

He had offended God. Now since the malice of an offense grows according to the one offended, notice how malicious *this* offense is. The one offended here is infinite, so the offense must be such also in some sense.

Now this is the heck of a situation to be in, because no man can satisfy for an infinite offense. Oh, we can make some feeble efforts at penitence to show we're sorry, but we simply don't have what it takes to make any *satisfaction* in this case.

God could, of course, have simply declared that the sin was forgiven, but this wouldn't satisfy for the sin either.

So now what?

We know now, historically, that God came up with a solution that only He could have thought up. Man had done the sinning, the offending. Therefore it was man who, somehow, had to make up for this sin. But God, an infinite Being, was the one offended. And so satisfaction for the sin had to be on God's level. The only possibility, then, of really satisfying for sin would have to come from both God and man. And so, in history, we had the Incarnation, by which God, the second Person of the Blessed Trinity, became Man, taking on a human nature. And this is the God-Man, Jesus Christ.

(I'd like to ask you to look back at Volume I of this series of books, *Learn a Little!*, to help you recall what Christ is like.)

Now all this sounds a little academic, so let's not forget one huge fact: the Incarnation and the Passion are for our redemption, sure, but along with that reason, Christ had another one — to show His love for us.

So God became Man, Christ, and came down to our earth, suffered and died for us. This is the Redemption. Man had sinned and the God-Man had redeemed him from the effects of that sin and made up for it as well.

But the Redemption isn't something that works automatically in an individual case. It's something that has to be *accepted* before an individual can be saved by it. Original sin has to be removed. So do mortal sins. Christ's Incarnation and Passion made this *possible*. But in order to actuate that possibility, something further is required.

Now we call the process of getting rid of original sin "justification." The Church has a somewhat lengthy definition of this word, but all the words are easy enough. So let's look at the definition: Justification is the transference from that state in which a man is born a son of the first Adam into the state of grace and adoption of the sons of God through the Second Adam, Jesus Christ our Savior.

We're born sons of the first Adam — therefore, in the state of original sin. But through the merits of Christ we're transferred into the state of grace. We become adopted sons of *God* instead of just sons of Adam.

You'll notice, if you're half awake, that Christ is referred to here as "the Second Adam." This is a pretty accurate title if you analyze it. Adam is the beginner of the human race; Christ re-begins it spiritually after Adam has, in a sense, destroyed it spiritually. Adam sinned; Christ makes up for that sin. "Oh God," we pray at the Offertory of the Mass, "who hast wonderfully created human nature and still more wonderfully renewed it . . ."

So how come anything else is necessary if Christ died for us? That looks like an *infinite* act — and that's enough justification for everybody.

Of course it's enough — more than enough. But suppose some character ignores it, or refuses to accept it, or will not even believe in the Redemption? After all, it doesn't make much sense to suppose that a man with an intellect and a free will could be redeemed automatically when he can keep his intellect from learning the truth and use his free will to turn away from God. No, the Redemption has to be applied to each person individually if it's to do him any good. The human race is not saved as a unit. Each one has a soul which is his alone, and which he's going to save or lose.

As you undoubtedly suspect, a person is "justified" at baptism. It is here that the Redemption is applied to the individual, so that the one baptized loses original and all other sin, and receives sanctifying grace and all the gifts that go with it — the adoption as children of God, being turned into temples of the Holy Spirit, and the gift of God's special friendship. With the sacrament of baptism we became justified, we were elevated to a supernatural level, so that if we had been lucky enough to die at that moment, we would have gone directly to heaven, nonstop.

(I suppose you could refer to the removal of an actual mortal sin in the confessional as a sort of "second justification," since it, too, is a transference from sin to grace. But let's stick with the definition as given, keeping this secondary meaning back in a quiet corner of our heads — even if only square heads have corners. Sorry. Let's continue.)

It is extremely important that we get a clear idea of what justification really is, of just what is involved in the process. Mistakes about the nature of this word have caused tremendous harm throughout history, harm which could have been avoided, very often, by unemotionalized, calm, objective thought.

And first of all, justification could not involve God's "shutting His eyes" to reality, to the fact of our having sinned. How could an all-knowing God pretend that something real did not exist! And yet, this "doctrine" has been taught by some who were too wrapped up in their own problems and their own emotions to let their intellects function properly.

No, justification is something much more serious and more definite than this. It contains two elements — a positive and a negative element. At baptism, when Christ's Redemption is applied to us, sin is *removed* from our souls, original sin and every other kind. (And just why should an all-powerful God have to "cover up" something He can remove? His suffering must have been worth more than a cover!) This you might call the negative element. Positively, at baptism, sanctifying grace is infused into our souls as the principle of our supernatural life. Your soul, you know, is called the principle of your *natural* life, the *source* of your life, that because of which you live and without which you die. And in the same way, you live or die supernaturally by the presence or absence of sanctifying grace. *This* is justification, then — the removal of sin and the infusion of a supernatural principle, grace. We'll have more to say about grace soon.

Now, infants are sort of unique in this matter of justification. And since most of you readers are a few years past infancy, maybe we'd better be practical and talk about those of you who may even have passed into the age of reason by this time.

For an adult, there are a number of things which have to precede justification. And, among these, faith takes first place.

Now there's been just as much ink spilled about this little word *faith* as about justification. Not only that, but often enough the ink has splashed with all the logical clarity of one of those ink-blot tests you see in psychiatrists' offices. Let's try to get a few clear ideas on the subject.

It's important, first of all, that we realize that faith is not a *feeling*. As soon as you come up with a blooper like calling faith a feeling, you've already messed up your intellect and are well on the way to warping a few emotions too. If faith were a feeling, then we'd always have to feel good when experiencing it. Suppose, for instance, you went to Mass or Holy Communion or confession, and you felt dry and low and unimpressed about it all. That would mean that on those occasions you had no faith, no matter how much you realized, intellectually, the depth of meaning of these sacraments. And it would mean that the lack of such a feeling would completely invalidate, for instance, your confession.

Now that just doesn't make sense — that you'd have to

feel good about a thing before it would be considered worthy or meritorious or connected with faith at all. You can't always *feel* good about getting up early for Mass, or about keeping the moral law, or about passing up some occasion of sinful pleasure, or even about an act of faith itself. How horrible always to have to feel good about God's existence and how easily such a necessity could lead to despair!

But how different is the true concept of faith from this sort of vaporizing. Faith cannot be just a feeling. This would mean that we would have to work our way to heaven with our emotions. No, faith can rather be defined as "an intellectual assent by which, with the help of God and His grace we believe what He has revealed, not because it is perceived as true by natural reason, but because of the authority of God revealing." This and nothing else is the act of faith.

An "intellectual assent" is by no means an emotion. It's an act of one of our highest faculties, which concerns thought and not feeling. In other words, we consent, say, to the fact that God exists not because we *feel* it or feel good about it, but because we're intellectually convinced of it.

Second, however, although faith is an *intellectual* assent, it is, nevertheless, performed "with the help of God and His grace." A merely intellectual assent *un*accompanied by God's grace would be only a natural act and so could not be a supernatural act of faith. Therefore, both elements have to be there — both our intellectual assent and the help of God's grace. And how different this is from some vague feeling! You can make an act of faith at any time — no matter *how* you feel.

The object of faith is stated very clearly in this definition also. We believe, in the act of faith, "what He has revealed." And so, an act by which we express the belief that two and two are four is not a supernatural act of faith because it's not something God has revealed.

Finally, when we make a supernatural act of faith, our

motive for the act is not only our natural reason but God's authority as well. In other words, although we might know a thing from reason also, still, in an act of supernatural faith, our motive is not so much our human reason as the fact that God tells us so and that God, who is all truth and all wisdom and goodness, would not reveal anything false. Now this isn't blindness or anything resembling it — it's the strongest kind of certitude there is. After all, only the fool would fail to believe something which God tells him.

Let's get another thing straight here, too — faith is not the blind act of belief in something our intellect tells us is contradictory. It goes hand in hand with reason. Not that our intellect can always figure it out perfectly, but the intellect can't show an object of faith to be contradictory either.

Faith, then, is one of the prerequisites for justification. There are others, but this is the big one. Let's make sure of one very important point here, however — important as faith is, it isn't enough for your salvation. You have to *act* in accord with your faith, too!

Now these are some pretty heady things we've been discussing here — the Redemption, justification, faith. They are, I'm afraid, truths which you simply can't grasp by just reading. As a matter of fact, you can't understand them fully by merely thinking about them either. But you will get a lot of enlightenment on these truths if you not only think about them but pray about them as well. You might try that now for a few minutes.

Think of the Redemption and of how Christ died for us. Without this, you and I would be doomed to hell. Think of how you're applying this Redemption to yourself. Think of what faith and justification really mean. And ask God, the Source of all these things, to make them clear to you. He'll do so — but He does want you to *ask*.

chapter III

"GOD AND I CAN DO ANYTHING!"

Probably from the first day you began to dog-ear a penny catechism with your grubby little fingers, you were told that there are two kinds of grace — sanctifying and actual. And undoubtedly your uncompromising little mind came up with some penetrating question like "Oh?" Let's try to answer that question now, even though it is a little subtle.

If you examine the various creatures in the world around you, you will probably discover that you can fit them all into several general classes. Depending on your viewpoint, you could probably say that the lowest class of creature might be something like a rock. It has no life. It can't think, can't eat, can't do anything. Not that it's stupid, but it simply has no capability of being anything else but a rock. That's its nature — to lie there.

If you go up a step in this hierarchy of creatures, you come to plant life — a tree or a squash or something like that. Now these things are on a somewhat higher level than a rock. At least they're capable of one or two little accomplishments that would stump any rock. A plant, for instance, can take in nourishment. It can grow. It can reproduce its own kind. These things are proper to its nature.

On a still higher level of being you find those creatures who have sensitive life. You usually call them animals. And an animal has all the attributes the two lower classes of creatures have — plus a few other things. A dog can lie around — like a rock. He can take in nourishment, grow, and reproduce his own kind — like a plant. He can see and hear and taste and touch and smell. (Transitive verb here.) He can wag his tail or even chase it if he enjoys that sort of recreation, and he can bark up a storm if that pleases him. He has these tremendously wonderful things called the senses, and so *his* nature is not just to grow and vegetate, but to see and taste and so on, as well.

But let's go up one more step, above the animals, and here we run into *human* nature. Man possesses, of course, all the perfections of those natures below him. He can — and often does — lie around like a rock. He eats and grows and is capable of reproducing his own kind. He can see and hear. Now, it may be true that a lot of human beings spend most of their time being vegetables or animals, but it is also true that man is capable of much more than this — he can think and he can freely *choose.* So his nature is essentially above that of the rocks and plants and animals.

Often enough, when we do think, we don't think deeply enough, and we tend to imagine that there couldn't possibly be any being higher than ourselves. There is, though, even if we don't see too many of this variety on the street. They're called angels. An angel has all the perfections of a man's nature with very few of the drawbacks. An angel is a pure spirit, with an intellect and will, but without any body to get in the way. An angel is by nature an intellectual being, a spiritual being, and therefore essentially higher in nature than a man.

But, of course, at the very top of the hierarchy of being, not just essentially above the other classes of being but *infinitely* above them, is God. So all these natures differ *essentially* from each other — and that's quite a difference. But, the distance between God's nature and any of the others is more than essential — it's infinite, a distance that is limitless, unbounded, and could never be bridged.

Now what's the reason for this long digression? Well, I used the word *natural* pretty often, so a shrewd guess might lead you to the conclusion that we're going to talk about the "*super*natural." *Super* is a word that does creep into your vocabulary occasionally, so you shouldn't have much trouble with it. You use it to mean something really good, something better, something real cool, or nervous, or george, or the like. But, literally, it means simply *above* something. And so, *super*natural means *above* nature. Now let's apply this to that hierarchy of being we talked about. Take a rock, for instance. Its nature is just to lie around and be a rock. But if, somehow or other, you could give that rock the ability to sprout leaves or to grow, you'd be giving it some powers supernatural to it, abilities *above* its nature. Or take a plant — a tree, say — and endow it somehow with the ability to see or walk. You would be giving that tree something above its nature, something *super*natural to it.

Let's move up a step. Suppose you have a dog — a very wonderful animal, as all dogs are. (If you think you detect a slight prejudice, you do.) You teach him all kinds of tricks — like collecting all the neighborhood newspapers, for instance. But suppose that some day you teach him, not just to collect the newspapers, but to read them to you. You've taught that pooch a trick essentially above his nature. You've given him something supernatural to him. (And, in the state he's supposedly in, don't be surprised if he thanks you.)

By this time, the meaning of "supernatural" should be more than obvious to you. Now, apply it to yourself. You and I can perform actions which are *natural* to us, but we can't perform actions above our nature any more than a dog can read newspapers or a squash can bark. We can't perform actions supernatural to us. However, when we were baptized, we entered into the state of sanctifying grace, which means that *God elevated us to His own level, to the level of His own nature*. If you could elevate a dog's nature to that of a human being, that would be tremendous, because this would bridge an essential gap. But when God elevates us to the level

If you can teach your dog to cook, for instance, you will be elevating him far above his nature.

of *His* nature (and this He *really* does, through sanctifying grace, while any question of elevating a dog is completely academic), He is bridging an *infinite* gap, and not just an essential one. The unelevated human being, the one not in the state of sanctifying grace, can perform only the actions of a human being, in accord with his nature. But if God elevates this person to the level of His own nature, by sanctifying grace, he will then be able to perform actions which are really like those of God. Outside of the state of sanctifying grace, you can perform some very nice human actions, but they're natural to you and by no means *above* your nature.

In other words, they won't get you to heaven. But when God elevates you by sanctifying grace, you enter into a *super*natural realm, and you're able to perform actions which are Godlike and meritorious. Your whole nature has been elevated.

It's always kind of nice, when you're discussing a certain topic, to decide, somewhere along the line, just how you'd define the subject under discussion. And it's high time we got some idea of what "sanctifying grace" means.

The two-bit definition of sanctifying grace goes like this: It's a created supernatural gift, distinct from actual graces, abiding physically and permanently, a spiritual quality inhering in the soul as a new nature and really distinct from the Holy Spirit and the habit of charity.

Now *there* is a mouthful! But let's chew it a little.

It's a *created* gift — of course.

It's *supernatural*. If you don't dig that word by now, slam the book shut.

It's *distinct from actual graces,* because, as you're going to see, actual grace is simply a short, supernatural help of God and sanctifying grace is a permanent state we live in.

It abides physically and permanently in the soul. It's a *quality*. Easy enough. Sanctifying grace is in you and not in the chandelier — that's "physically." If you don't understand "permanently," maybe you'd better check the dictionary.

It abides *as a new nature*. You see any connection between that and the word *supernatural* above? If you don't, well . . . Somehow, I just don't know how to end that sentence.

Sometimes a definition can be a pretty cold proposition. So let's see if we can't *describe* sanctifying grace a little bit instead of just speculating on the definition. Everything in this description will come, at least indirectly, from the definition itself.

Most obviously, sanctifying grace confers on us a new nature, just as the definition says. We have always had a human nature. With sanctifying grace we gain a share in the nature of God.

You may or may not remember that when we defined justification it had to do with our becoming sons of God, through Christ. Now, if you analyze that somewhat, you'll see that we can't be sons of God by reason of our own nature, but must be elevated above our nature. Since this is true, and since Christ is the only *natural* Son of God, we must be *adopted* sons of God.

You know pretty well what adoption is. A young couple checks in with the adoption agency and then, maybe, they look over the babies at the local orphanage and decide on the one or more they would like to adopt. Notice the obvious, though — they always adopt a *child,* a *human being*. You do not *adopt* an animal, like a dog for instance. You buy one, or you help him to follow you home, but you don't "adopt" him. You only adopt someone of your own nature. With sanctifying grace, however, God can't adopt anyone of His own nature because He, and only He, is infinite. And so, in adopting us, He not only adopts us, but in that very act He elevates us to His own nature. That's the main difference between God's adopting us and human adoption.

If God gives us a new nature in sanctifying grace, adopting us as His children, then this must mean that we're being given a new *life*. This concept ties in perfectly with the other ideas we've been outlining here. You see, while you live on a natural level before sanctifying grace comes into your soul, you begin a new life, on a level infinitely above your natural powers, once this grace does come to you.

I suppose you could sum up the total effect of sanctifying grace by saying that we live in a state of *friendship* with God when we are in this state. You see, God is in a tree or a rock or an animal — keeping them in existence. But He is in you, by sanctifying grace, *as a Friend*. Without Sanctifying Grace, then, God's presence in you is not really much more intimate than His presence in a tree or a cat. But when you are in the state of grace, He is with you as a Friend. Do you begin, perhaps, to see how horrible mortal sin is — when it can reduce you to the level of an animal or a plant or even a rock (or lower, in fact)? And do you get a small hint here, maybe, of what it might mean to be a "temple of God," so that God dwells in you by grace?

You know, these are terribly important thoughts, terribly deep thoughts, and, in fact, almost terrifying thoughts. In fact, probably the best thing you could do right now is close the book and think and pray a little about these tremendous facts. Make them vivid for yourself. Can you ever, even with your greatest efforts, exhaust the idea that you, at this moment, are the temple of God and that God *dwells* in you?

But there's another kind of grace, too, one that can make a tremendous difference in our lives. Again, this is not a new term in your vocabulary — this actual grace — but it may be a term that's still somewhat vague to you. So let's get some idea of what it's like.

And first of all, where sanctifying grace is a permanent state or condition, actual grace is only a relatively short supernatural help that God gives us. But it's not just any old help, either, not even just any of God's helps to us. You see, God helps you to stay alive and act and so on, but these things are not properly actual grace. Actual grace is not a help given to win a basketball tournament or anything like that. It's a *supernatural* help, one that helps us to gain or stay in the state of sanctifying grace, or to get closer to God.

There is a variety of such graces, of course, and, unfortunately, we probably pass up a variety of them, every day. The two big general types of such graces are external and internal.

An external actual grace is simply some outside influence for good which comes to us in God's Providence. A good sermon can be such a help if you don't sleep through it. The good example of some of your companions could be one. Even bad example with God's help and guidance, could lead to an actual grace, because God can bring good out of evil. Even this book you're reading now might be such a grace for you. At least it's intended to be.

But an external actual grace isn't really in the same category as internal actual grace. It's more an influence than anything else. Internal actual grace is really something supernatural, and it can best be defined in this way: It's a transient, supernatural help of God to avoid sin or to perform some salutary act, and it consists in an illumination of the intellect and an inspiration of the will. Now let's re-check that definition step-by-step. Probably the best way of clarifying it will be by describing the way an actual grace will usually operate.

"Transient," of course, means passing or temporary. You know that already.

There must be hundreds of extraordinary ways that grace can operate. Some of them are a little violent, perhaps, like St. Paul's getting knocked off his horse and being blinded. Usually grace works a bit more gently than this.

Ordinarily, it operates a little less sensationally. Into your intellect will come an indeliberate act of some sort, an act vital to your intellect but nevertheless not put there by yourself. Such an act can properly be called an illumination of your intellect. The light has been turned on. Next, you would probably become conscious that such an act was present there, and so you'd make it your own. Another way of putting this would be to call the act indeliberate at first and then deliberate. Third, you make some judgment about this act that's present in your mind. You decide, let's say, that this is a good act, that it's prompting you to perform some act of virtue, a good act. At about this stage in the working of an actual grace, there would be an inspiration of your will, the urge or impulse to act on this idea. Then, finally, you will make some choice about the matter — to act or not to act.

You're completely free — you can always accept a grace or refuse it.

Now let's trace this process with an example. Suppose you are free during your lunch hour, and the thought occurs to you to drop into a church or a chapel for a visit. This thought came into your mind spontaneously, let's say, without your willing it. Then a moment comes when you realize the idea is there and you make it your own. It becomes deliberate.

Once this stage is reached, you have to make some sort of judgment about the idea. In this case, you'd probably judge that it would be a good thing to visit Christ in the Blessed Sacrament. And together with this judgment comes God's inspiration, encouraging you to act on this grace and to make a visit to the chapel. Finally, you can choose either to go into the chapel and make a visit or you can choose not to. You can either accept this grace or you can reject it. And so God's illumination of your intellect and inspiration can be, and often is, I'm afraid, completely frustrated by your free choice. Of course, your salvation may depend on how you choose. Or your sanctification may depend on it. And either one is of tremendous importance.

That's pretty much the way actual grace will *ordinarily* work. Undoubtedly, God can use His own grace as He wishes. But I'll bet if you would look back on your life a little bit, you'd find that the process I've just described has gone on often in your life. And, probably, all too often you've made the wrong decision and refused God's grace. Another very important thing to remember here is that grace works in a *series* — so that if you refuse one grace, there's no guarantee at all that you'll get another one. But more of that later.

The important thing to figure out now is just what *good* this actual grace is. How important and how necessary is it? To answer that, let's try to remember, first of all, just how much you and I depend upon God — and this for absolutely

No matter how good *an act we perform, it can't be supernatural or meritorious without God's grace.*

everything, not just for our supernatural life but for our natural life and our very existence as well. Keep in mind that if God were to stop thinking about you at this moment, you wouldn't just die, but you'd go out of existence. And, over and above that, keep in mind that you couldn't perform a single action without God's co-operation.

But even more important than this is the fact that we can't perform a single *supernatural* action without God's help. How could we? We're on the level of our own natures, just as a rock is on its level and a plant on its level. And we can't rise above our own nature any more than a pumpkin can suddenly start chasing a cat. We have a supernatural destiny, though, one infinitely beyond our reach, above our nature. And we'll *have* to perform supernatural actions to accomplish it. Therefore, we *have* to have God's grace, too.

Isn't it funny how often we've told ourselves that as soon as we want to change our lives, we'll do so? How often we've figured we'll make a good confession, or even outdistance the saints — when *we* decide to do so! Of course, that isn't quite true. In fact, it isn't true at all. Good will is fine, but we have to have God's grace along with it before we can do anything like this. *We can do absolutely nothing on a supernatural level without God's grace.*

Now we know that any salutary (or meritorious) act we perform has to be a supernatural act. And we know, too, that such an act is infinitely above our natures. That means that we're *physically* incapable of performing such an act. It would be like trying to see without eyes or talk without a tongue. But Christ put it better than anyone else could: "As the branch cannot bear fruit of itself unless it remain on the vine, so neither can you unless you abide in me . . . without me you can do nothing" (Jn. 15:4, 5). Pretty clear, huh?

Not only can't we perform a supernatural act without God's grace — we can't even keep the natural law very long without it. Again, here is something we tell ourselves, perhaps, that we can handle all by ourselves, but the fact is that we really can't do it by ourselves. St. Paul put this very simply: ". . . I do not the good that I wish, but the evil that I do not wish, that I perform" (Rom. 7:19).

Now if you examine deeply enough this inability to keep the natural law, you will see that it's not what you would call a physical inability (like the performance of a supernatural action), but rather a moral one. It's simply that the difficulties of keeping this law are far too enormous for a human being over the long haul, that he needs outside help if he is going to keep this law for any length of time. It's like the typist who could, physically, type hundreds of pages without a single mistake, but who is morally incapable of perfection so consistent.

Along this same line, it's morally impossible, too, that someone in the state of mortal sin should keep from further mortal sin without actual grace. Physically and absolutely, it could be done. Morally, it's impossible. But with God's help, of course, nothing is impossible.

Not only that, but this same person — the guy in the state of mortal sin — can't get back to God, into the state of sanctifying grace, without the help of actual grace. So this is his situation: he can neither keep away from further mortal sin nor can he get out of that state without God's grace. So he'd better get some grace or he's sunk.

Even the person in the state of sanctifying grace has great need of God's actual grace. He can't persevere in that state too long without actual grace, for one thing. And over and above that, if a person can't stay in the state of grace long without actual grace, he certainly couldn't die in that state without grace either. Final perseverance (dying in the state of sanctifying grace) is a tremendous *gift,* one we just can't attain without God's special help.

So, without Him we can do nothing. True. But let's not stop there. Let's never forget that *with* Him we can do anything. And let's not forget, either, that, while we need grace so badly and so completely, God *will* give it to us.

First of all, we know perfectly well that God *wants* everyone to be saved. That's why He created everyone in the first place. It is only a man himself who, going against God's will, can condemn himself to eternal punishment, despite the fact that God wills his salvation.

And a second fact which goes with this one is a simple conclusion that anyone can make — that if God wants everyone to be saved, then He must give everyone the means of salvation. Add a third fact to that — that you know that grace is the only means of salvation — and you have to realize that God gives every man sufficient grace to be saved.

Check back on the things you need grace for — to perform any supernatural act, to stay out of sin, to persevere. Tie them in with *this* conclusion and you have more knowledge of this subject. God *will* give everyone the grace to perform supernatural actions. He *will* give the grace to avoid sin or get out of sin. And he *will* give the grace of final perseverance. After all, even the sin of Judas was pardonable until he gave in to final despair. Maybe good people have to be more careful than others on this particular point, because if they should sometimes fall into sin, their tendency might be to become so ashamed as to give up, to give in to a type of despair, forgetting that no sin is unforgivable except the sin of saying that God will not forgive them.

The big thing is, then, in general, that God gives everyone enough grace to be saved. Theologians who have devoted their lives to figuring out things like this say that, practically and remotely, this is going to take the form of the grace to *pray*. I mentioned that this is the *remote* grace to be saved, because, while God has to give everyone the grace to be saved, He doesn't have to give them any *more* than that minimum grace. So, going on from there, let's suppose that God gives George the grace to pray, a grace, which, if accepted, will lead to other graces, and, ultimately, to the salvation of George's soul. And suppose George is "too busy" to accept this first grace. Maybe he's doing something very important like walking the dog or spinning some very important platters or something world-shaking like that. George has passed up the remote grace of salvation, and there's no guarantee he'll ever be given another one. On the other hand if old George accepts this grace to pray, God will give him a further grace, the whole series leading to his salvation. One grace leads to another. (This isn't to say that God *won't* give us further graces, disregarding our stupidity and willfulness and haziness in passing up grace. But there's nothing which says He *has* to, no absolute guarantee He will.)

The fact that the remote grace of salvation is the grace to pray gives us a pretty good hint of the way to get grace. We get it through prayer. And, naturally, we get it through the sacraments. We're going to talk about these two tremendous sources of grace in the next chapter.

Maybe we'd better relax for a minute, though, and try

to remember where we've been and where we are. That *should* make it a little easier to see where we're going.

We have a purpose, a single purpose — to get to God in heaven. We miss that, and we've missed the whole boat. Moreover, it's a supernatural purpose — one so far above us, we could never reach it by ourselves. But God doesn't expect us to reach it by ourselves. He offers us His grace — sanctifying and actual — to help us. He makes us His children, in fact, raising us to His level. And He offers us the further help of actual grace — if we'll only ask for it.

Think a little. Pray a little. And then let's go on to the next chapter and see how we go about getting His grace and increasing it in our souls.

chapter IV

GRACE IS YOURS FOR THE ASKING

If grace is so important, and if we get it chiefly through prayer and the sacraments, it might do us some good to look into these two things and see what they're like. Let's start with prayer.

Now just what is prayer? It must be hard to define, because so many of the "definitions" you see fall so short of perfection. We won't be able to come up with a perfect definition here, either.

Prayer has been called speaking with God. And that's a nice idea, even a beautiful idea, but it doesn't tell you exactly what prayer is. Prayer has also been called listening to God, and that doesn't do the job either because that leaves it almost completely passive. But both of these definitions have elements of truth in them, and so if you combine the two, you come up with a pretty good working definition of prayer. Speaking to God and listening to Him would mean you're having a "conversation with God." And that isn't a bad definition of prayer.

Not bad, true, but it's not a perfect definition either. A better definition still, if we understand it properly, would be "union with God," or, in St. Augustine's words, "the soul's affectionate quest of God."

Those are all pretty fair definitions and, while none of them is a perfect definition, each one gives you a piece of an idea of what prayer really is. Maybe we can learn a little more about it, though, if we take a look at the different *kinds* of prayer.

Prayer isn't just talking to God — it's listening *to Him, too.*

You might say that vocal prayer is at the bottom of the heap of prayer. That doesn't mean it isn't any good — it's just at the bottom. Now vocal prayer is not necessarily *oral* prayer. Otherwise, you could not pray vocally in church without driving your neighbors out of their respective minds.

Vocal prayer is not necessarily oral prayer.

Maybe you've had the tough luck to find yourself in church sometime in front of someone who believes in reciting his prayers not just to God but to you also. Well, that wasn't just vocal prayer — it was oral prayer. In fact it may not have been "vocal prayer" at all. No, vocal prayer is simply prayer which uses a set form of words. So when you say a "Hail Mary," or an "Our Father," you are praying vocally, whether you shout these prayers or say them silently.

A somewhat higher type of prayer is what is called meditation. Probably most people who have never tried it think that meditation is something very difficult. It isn't though — it's fairly easy. Meditation means simply taking a certain truth — a revealed truth, perhaps — thinking it out, and then praying about it. It's as simple as that. To show how easy it is, let's take an example of how it works.

Take a simple truth like this one: "God so loved the world that He gave His only-begotten Son." Suppose you want to meditate on this idea. First, you ask yourself a series of questions. It's a good idea to have such a series in mind if you intend to do much praying — questions like Who? What? Why? With what love? Notice, for instance, how you can apply them to this particular truth. For instance, ask yourself the question, Who? Who is God? Who is His only-begotten Son? Who falls under the heading of "the world"? To the question, What? you'd answer that God loved us, that He gave us His Son — on the cross. Now put all these answers together. Compare yourself with God. Even so, He loves us — far out of proportion. You simply can't put facts like those together and not come up with some sort of prayer. Certain acts of your will occur almost spontaneously — acts of faith in God, sorrow that you've been such a heel, humility, confidence, and hope in One who has done so much for us, thanksgiving for His doing so much, and love for One who loves us despite ourselves.

So you see, this meditating process isn't really tough at all. A few reasonable questions to warm up the intellect, and we pray almost spontaneously. There's enough matter for prayer in just those few little ideas above to keep you going for a long, long time. And that's meditation. Try it for a few minutes. And then make a habit of it — a few minutes a day. Keep in mind some such set of questions as are given above and a working-list of acts of the will, too. With these in mind, you're ready to meditate. If you try it and stick with it, you're in for some pleasant surprises. If you don't, you'll never know what you've missed. One thing you will have missed, of course, is the genuine joy one can have in getting closer to God (the Source of all love and beauty, remember?) — a sort of foretaste of heaven.

But let's not exaggerate the joys of prayer. They're real, sure, but you have to struggle sometimes to experience them — as you do with anything worthwhile, of course. It will usually happen that a person will begin to meditate and experience some thrill in doing so, largely because of the novelty of the process and because of God's custom of making it as easy as possible for us at first. But as time goes on, the novelty wears off, and God puts us a little more on our own. And with the passing of His special helps, we experience a dryness or aridity. If we get discouraged at this point, we're all through as far as prayer is concerned. But if we stick it out, fight it through when the going gets tough, do all we can to keep going, then we're going to get somewhere. This aridity, you see, is a test God lets you go through to see if you're worthy of growing into closer union with Him. You can either pass or flunk.

Apart from your own good sense and courage, there are other sources of help for you. If you're really serious about this all-important thing called prayer, you can get some expert help on it by reading about it and asking someone who knows a little bit about it to help you with your own personal prayer problems. Such a person — a priest, for instance — can tell you whether dryness in prayer is your own fault or not. And he can offer suggestions for dealing with it.

If you do manage to persevere in prayer, you'll probably find that you are gradually leaving out the intellectual side of the process — the Who? and What? and such — and getting right at the affections, at acts of faith and sorrow and the like. And the more you begin to do this, the more you are getting right into the heart of prayer, and the closer you are coming to what is called "affective prayer." Affective prayer is simply meditation without the emphasis on the acts of the intellect. It consists more in acts of the will, acts of faith and hope and the love of God. In other words, it's more thoroughly "prayer" than meditation is.

Father Walter Farrell, O.P., who wrote many wonderful things, the most wonderful, perhaps, his *Companion to the Summa,* tells about a lady who came to him for some advice on prayer. She used to drop in to visit Christ in the Blessed Sacrament during her noon hour each working day. But she complained to Father that whenever she knelt in the church and began the "Hail Mary," she became so engrossed with the goodness of Christ before her in the Blessed Sacrament that she was never able to finish the "Hail Mary" by the time she had to go back to work. And she was griping that she couldn't pray!

Maybe this affective prayer is a kind you should try, particularly in your visits to the Blessed Sacrament. Don't think you have to fire a lot of words at Christ. If that were the case, you could pray best by reading a dictionary to Him, and not even your merely human friends are going to stand still for *that*. No, just go into the church and, especially if you're tired, just look at the tabernacle and think of who's present before you. That's plenty. Let God take it from there. Prayer is not just a speech. It's not a double monologue either. It's the soul's affectionate quest of God. It's union with Christ.

There are other, higher types of prayer, but they're gifts of God, depending not so much on our own efforts as on God's decision to favor us with them. Such a form of prayer is one called "loving attention to God," which seems to be built on affective prayer, with God helping along more than usual. It would consist mostly in faith and love of God — simpler than affective prayer. And the more God enters the picture, the simpler it becomes. Naturally, God *is* simplicity. Only human beings complicate things.

The final type of prayer that I should mention here is "infused contemplation." The main reason for bringing it in here is for completeness, and also to make sure your ideas on it are clear and correct. And, first of all, this type of prayer is an absolute gift. Either God gives it or no one gets it. But, on the other hand, it's not a gift that He gives to only one person per century. It's not *that* rare.

Infused contemplation is a single view of eternal truth, without reasoning, and accompanied by great love and admiration of God. That's it. So don't get it mixed up with anything miraculous. It's not. Nor is it a vision nor an ecstasy nor being raised off the ground nor anything like these things. No, the recipients of this gift can continue to lead very active lives in the world of business or in the religious life or in whatever state they live.

The single view of eternal truth that is infused contemplation can take place in a very few seconds, and even in this short space a person could know more about some attribute or aspect of God than if he had studied theology for years. It's a view which is simple, momentary, and perfectly clear.

Strangely enough, the person who has this gift will not always be completely aware that he has it. And this is where a spiritual adviser is so important. He can spot it where no one else could, and he can distinguish it from other things too. This is an extremely important point, because we can really fool ourselves easily in a matter like this. Don't worry about infused contemplation. If God wants you to have it, you will have. Otherwise you won't. So leave that to Him — entirely.

Probably, you can draw your own practical conclusions from just the description of these types of prayer. Certainly, you should pray vocally, when for example you use a missal at Mass or when you say your Rosary. But even vocal prayer shouldn't be like a mathematical formula, and so you should be thoughtful and prayerful as you read or recite the words. Don't dash through *any* prayers, vocal or otherwise, but think of them as you go. It is, for instance, much better for you to spend a little thoughtful time on one prayer at Mass than to rush like mad through the whole missal. Thought is important even to vocal prayer.

Secondly, we should all try to meditate, not just once, but regularly. If you try it once and then let it go until you happen to think of it again, you're not going to get too far with it. But if you set aside five to fifteen minutes a day for meditation (the same time every day is best) and stick with it, you'll get somewhere. Meditation may start out easy, but it doesn't always stay that way. It takes some courage. But, with courage, it can be tremendous.

Thirdly, you should be willing, once you've begun to meditate, to let affective prayer take over your meditations, so that acts of your will, acts of the love of God and so forth, rather than intellectual gymnastics, predominate. And always, no matter how you pray, keep asking for God's help.

Finally, with God's help, we can simplify even this affective prayer, and so come closer all the time to a real union with God. From here on, of course, our progress is going to depend more and more on God. We must always do our part, and God will do His. Stick with that old principle: "Work as if everything depends upon yourself, and pray as if everything depends upon God." You can't go wrong if you follow that.

Now there's no use stopping with some vague general terms and nice ideas about prayer. We can dream about prayer all our lives and never learn anything about it. We may even look longingly toward that great gift of God, infused contemplation, wishing while we could be praying.

Let's see, rather, how prayer can work into the ordinary, everyday life, and, seeing that, let's try to figure what God has in mind for us with regard to prayer.

Christ gave us some rather startling instructions when He said we should "pray always." That would make it remarkably simple, except that we can hardly be expected to spend all day on our knees in prayer. After all, we have our lives to lead, and we have to make a living.

It really isn't very hard to see what He meant, if we honestly *try* to see. Obviously, He could not have meant that we are to pray — and nothing else — all day and all night. He expects us to live as human beings are supposed to live, with the right amount of time set apart for work and recreation, for eating and drinking and sleeping and everything else. But He did say to pray always, so He must have meant that we try to make absolutely everything we do a prayer. After all, prayer is ultimately union with God, and there's no reason we can't be united with God in even our most ordinary actions. There's no reason that we shouldn't gain merit from recreation as well as from acts of penance, voluntary or otherwise. (Naturally, a somewhat unpleasant thing like penance is going to take a little more courage and self-sacrifice than recreation is. But if it's God's will that we take a certain amount of recreation — and it is — then taking recreation must be meritorious.)

So, in order to pray always, we have to make all our actions prayerful. Probably the best way of doing that is by beginning each day with the Morning Offering, in which we offer all our "prayers, works, joys, and sufferings" of that day to God. Naturally, as the day goes on, we should renew this intention, so that we remind ourselves that we are doing everything for God. This is a good first step in following Christ's command to "pray always."

If we look around, we'll find time for a little more formal prayer — vocal prayer or meditation or affective prayer. We can, for instance, quite easily, get into the habit of saying our morning and evening prayers. There's no set formula for these, nothing you have to say. Nor do you have any serious obligation whatsoever to say these prayers at all. But there is at least one thing you should keep in mind with regard to morning and evening prayers — since they *are* things which are not binding under pain of sin, things we do of our own good, free will or not at all, therefore God is most probably going to reward us a hundredfold for even this little indication of good will on our part.

Now you may think this is just a pious platitude, but it's not. Certainly any priest can tell you that people who are faithful about such tiny little items as morning and evening prayers frequently are not bothered as much by temptations, and do not give in as often to temptation as others do. It's a rather remarkable thing that the boy who is willing to take time out each morning to get on his knees and say one *good* "Hail Mary," and who is willing and wise enough to get on his knees at night for just the space of an act of perfect contrition, simply has more success in conquering temptation than someone else who doesn't have enough energy and spirit of sacrifice to give these few seconds, morning and evening, exclusively to God. So don't consider these morning and evening prayers insignificant. They're not. If you have to, you can even say them as you wash or as you prepare for bed at night. But it's a lot better idea to get on your knees for these few seconds. You're not *that* busy!

There really aren't many of you who haven't *any* chance of getting to daily Mass and receiving Holy Communion daily. We're going to talk more about these things when we discuss the sacraments, but while we're on the subject of prayer, we can't leave out the greatest prayer we have, the Mass. Nowhere else, in fact, can we fulfill all our prayerful obligations to God — the obligation we have of adoring Him, of being sorry for our sins, of thanking Him and of asking for His grace. Think back here to the things we had to say about the Redemption, and you'll recall that only Christ can make satisfaction for sin. Remember, too, that in the Mass we offer God Himself to God, so when we combine these acts with God's infinite sacrifice — but *you* draw the obvious conclusion from these facts.

A little honesty will, I think, force you to admit that you could get to Mass very frequently — if you tried. You could also find many opportunities to drop into a church for a short visit to Christ — if you tried. Those of you who are still lucky enough to be in school certainly have such an opportunity, because you either go to school very close to a church or you will pass by one on your way home. Those of you who work probably pass by a church on your way to or from work. And there isn't *always* an insuperable parking problem. It would often be quite easy for you to drop in for at least a short visit to Christ in the Blessed Sacrament. This would be about the best time for you to make your meditation for that day, when it's just you and Christ alone together. Some days you'll be tired, sure. So, on those days, just sit there for five or ten minutes, looking at the tabernacle and trying to realize who is before you. If you can't think of anything else to say to Him, tell Him you're bushed. After all, He did say "Come to me, you who labor and are heavily burdened, and I will refresh you." There's no reason you shouldn't remind Him of this promise.

You Catholics who are reading this take Christ's Presence in the Blessed Sacrament so much for granted. And how many of you non-Catholics — if you did believe that Christ is actually present in the Blessed Sacrament — would not go in and at least say "Hello" every day? You Catholics should realize that you very frequently shock non-Catholics by the apparent contradiction between your actions and your belief. How, they ask, can Catholics say they believe that Christ is really present in their churches and then calmly and blindly pass by those churches time after time and day after day without going in? That's a good question. Maybe *you* can think of a good answer. I can't.

You have a rosary, surely. Instead of wasting the whole time daydreaming as you come home on the bus, why not

There are plenty of families who recite the Rosary together after dinner.

say your Rosary? You don't have to wave it before people's eyes and rattle the beads so that they'll know you're praying, but you can say it quietly and unobtrusively, keeping the beads in your pocket or just in your fist. It's simple. It's a beautiful prayer. And there's no reason we shouldn't say it every day. There are lots of families who recite the Rosary together right after dinner, sitting around the table or kneeling in the living room. Once you get the habit of saying it, it's easy. So why not get the habit?

Then there's an old custom at mealtime — saying grace before and after you eat, asking God to bless this food and then thanking Him for it. There are, after all, lots of people who either have no food, or don't have anything as good as what you get. So thank God for what He gives *you*.

Now that may seem a very small thing to you, but life is made up of small things. We're pretty small ourselves, as a matter of fact. No?

Those of you who attend Catholic schools have another

opportunity for prayer — in the prayers you say before and after class. Again, these are tiny things, but, tiny or not, they are reminders that the only worthwhile way to spend any day, the only good reason for going to class is for God. You know, come to think of it (*if* you think of it), even the short prayer before or after class could be one source of your salvation or sanctification!

Even in this day of television, they are still putting out things called "books." (They're sort of a hangover from those middle ages before your birth.) Not only that, but there *are* people who really enjoy reading these things. And in the realm of books today are some you might call "spiritual reading" books — lives of the saints, books on prayer and theology and the like. Now, don't go away — you might learn something.

You know, it used to be that many or most spiritual reading books *were* pretty corny, particularly the lives of the saints. But that day has definitely passed. There are great numbers of spiritual books today which are second to none in style and interest. Not only that, but there are spiritual books for every type of person — books for religious and lay people, for adults and teen-agers. Why, there are even "comic" spiritual books. So, you can take your choice — there are spiritual books, and good ones, to fit almost your every mood.

Now that may have seemed a pretty abrupt transition — from prayer to spiritual reading. It really wasn't a transition at all, though, because spiritual reading is — or can be — another form of prayer. But, like everything else, you have to try it before you find this out. Condemn it as "square" without trying it, and *you* end up the square.

Not that you're the first one who was ever revolted by the idea of reading a spiritual book. There was once a Spanish soldier named Iñigo who was so badly wounded that he had to spend a lot of time in bed. Since there wasn't any radio or TV in those days, he asked for some novels to read, to while away the time. But all the doctors and nurses could find were lives of the saints and of Christ. And so, to keep from going completely off his rocker, he picked these up and started to read. He expected to be completely bored, but he found, to his astonishment and delight, that he was far from bored. He began to be fascinated by the lives of the saints and, being the kind of guy he was, he began to ask himself "If these characters could do it, why can't I?" It was this question that started Iñigo, a tough worldly-minded soldier, on the path to becoming *St.* Ignatius, founder of the religious order called the Society of Jesus.

Another easy form of prayer is simply calling to mind God's presence in you as you go through your day. Keep His presence in mind, of course, and you'll remember that unless you act for Him, there's just no use acting at all. It would be my guess that the saints were people who thought frequently of God as they went through each day, and, thinking of Him, did His will as perfectly as possible — even down to drawing their next breath or taking their next step for Him, easily and without strain. So, the closer you can come to this ideal, doing God's will perfectly, the closer you'll come to sanctity — which is your real destiny. (A little thought here will show you why saints are the only really well-adjusted people there are. People only get maladjusted when they try to do their own wills, exclusively and selfishly.)

Now, naturally, keeping God in mind frequently throughout the day is going to have quite an influence on our actions. It will be hard, for instance, to do your homework sloppily and still claim to be doing it for God. Think of the things you omit every day, things which God really would want you to do. And think, too, of the things you sometimes do which are obviously not His will.

I wouldn't try to kid you into accepting the idea that

doing what God expects you to do is always an easy thing. It isn't. But it's not overwhelming, either, nor impossible.

But I started to talk about the *presence* of God and got sidetracked with the *will* of God. (And don't take *that* verb literally!) By now, you should know that God is present in you in several ways. He's present by His *power,* keeping you alive and helping you to perform your ordinary actions. Every breath you draw and every step you take has to be done with God's help or it can't be done at all. Your very existence, as I have pointed out already, depends on God at every moment. You've seen slide projectors, I'm sure, and you know that when the light goes out the picture stops. It's the same way with God's presence in you — should He stop thinking about you, you'd go out of existence. Luckily, He never forgets you for a moment.

But there's another way God is present in you and your companions — that is by sanctifying grace. He's present even in a tree by His power — keeping it in existence, but He's not present in a tree as a Friend, as He is in us by sanctifying grace. Now if you can keep in mind that God is present in you and your companions by sanctifying grace, making you a *temple* of God, you're doing what might be called some rather practical praying. And you can't help noticing the tremendous obstacle to sin this realization will bring. By your faith and prayer you know that sin isn't just the violation of some arbitrary law, but it's driving God and beauty out of your soul and maybe someone else's soul, and letting in ugliness and sin. It's as though you were to take one of the chalices used at Mass and step on it.

Think of this a little. Pray about it. Try meditating on it.

You know, one meaning of prayer is that we seek God rather than ourselves. Just for the heck of it, ask yourself seriously, at the end of the day, "What single action did I perform today that was not completely selfish? What did I do all day long for the motive of serving God or for helping someone else?" These can be some pretty embarrassing questions, because most of us lead our lives selfishly, not thinking of God or others, but thinking only of ourselves. But the road, not just to sanctity but to emotional stability as well, is one of *un*selfishness. Check it. Are you looking for yourself or for God? You have to pray to find *that* answer.

Naturally, all of this should be done without strain or tension. It should be perfectly natural for us to think of God and act for Him. Oh, we have to work at it. Sure. But effort is not the same as tension.

Another fairly easy way of praying is by rising to God through creatures, something that should become so natural to us that we do it automatically, because it is one of the best and easiest forms of prayer there is. If you look at a beautiful sunset in the mountains and see only sun and mountains, without connecting these things with the beauty of God, then you're not using your head. You should, in seeing a mountain or a flower or anything beautiful at all, be able to say almost automatically, "If God made something this beautiful, how much more beautiful must *He* be?" God's creatures are all around us — everything we see is one of his creatures. You girls, when you see a handsome boy, should be able to say — in the same breath in which you say "How cute!" — "and how much 'cuter' must God be." And you boys should be capable, not only of noticing the very real beauty of the female of the species, but also of having enough sense to know that God, her Creator, must be infinitely more lovely.

Gilbert Chesterton gave a hint of this in his usual clever way. "One elephant," he said, "with its absurd trunk is a wildly amusing sight. But for all elephants to have trunks suggests a conspiracy." And Father Leonard Feeney puts the matter equally well in one of the shortest poems in all literature: "Snails obey the holy / Will of God slowly."

You can't go to a zoo or an aquarium without realizing

some of the breadth of God's imagination and the facets of His beauty. Can you imagine God creating all the crazy-looking and intricate little insects and animals and fish, with all their varying degrees of attractive ugliness and cuteness? And can't you go backward in the process, so that when you see a bug, or a dog, or the beauty of a human being, you think of God? Of course you can. And that, chum, is praying.

These are only some of the very fundamental ideas about prayer. You're going to have to take it from here, do some research on it, study it, work at it, practice it. There's no substitute for practice, not even reading and study. You can acquire the greatest possible speculative knowledge of prayer and still be no good whatsoever at its practice. So combine the two. Learn about prayer. Practice it regularly. And you'll be using one of the two big sources of grace — as God expects you to.

When we pray, God gives us His grace — in accord with our good will and dispositions. But, when we receive the sacraments, we get His grace, not just according to our dispositions, but automatically, because of the particular sacrament itself as well. Each sacrament was, in fact, instituted to give a very definite kind of grace. The sacrament of baptism, for instance, was instituted to give us *sanctifying* grace, and, since it makes Christians out of us, the actual or sacramental grace to help us become *good* Christians. This is a grace peculiar to baptism.

It's the same way with the other sacraments — each one gives or increases sanctifying grace, and adds its own peculiar actual grace as well. Confirmation helps us to be *strong* Christians. The Holy Eucharist is the sacrament of Christ's love, so it shouldn't surprise you to find out that the peculiar grace of this sacrament is an increase of our love for God. Penance was instituted to take away sin and to help us avoid it, and these are the special graces we get from this very special sacrament. Holy Orders and matrimony are the sacraments of vocation, and so each one gives the grace to sanctify oneself in a particular state of life. Through the sacrament of extreme unction we'll get the grace to die a good death, to overcome the final temptations standing between us and God. Each sacrament, in other words, gives a grace peculiar to itself, a grace that you can get from no other source in that particular way and degree.

Even from this brief sketch, you can see how wonderful all the sacraments are. It would also be wonderful to be able to go through all of them in detail here. But that would add up to a whole book on the sacraments. And that isn't the purpose of *this* book. Besides, there already are a lot of good books and pamphlets on the sacraments. All you have to do is pick them up and read them. Try it sometime when you have nothing else to do. Or really shoot the works and do some such reading *instead* of something else!

All we'll have space for here is a pretty sketchy treatment of only two of the sacraments, the two we make use of most frequently — the sacraments of penance and the Holy Eucharist.

Even on these two sacraments, you'll probably not find anything new here. All I'd like to try in these pages is to simplify some of the ideas you already have on these sacraments, remind you of a few things you may have forgotten, and, hopefully, clarify a few other things. Let's begin with the sacrament of penance.

It's amazing at first, until you get a really deep knowledge of the personality of Christ, to notice His apparent preoccupation with sinners, almost to the exclusion of those he calls, seemingly with some irony, "the just." "I came," He says, "not to save the just, but sinners." Either the just are already saved, you see, or they're just only in their own eyes and are, like the Pharisees, too proud to be helped easily.

Christ is absorbed, moreover, with the salvation of not just the ordinary, garden variety of hidden sinner, but with the knock-'em-down-and-drag-'em-out type as well — the Mary Magdalene and Dismas types.

You don't, of course, show an attitude like that of Christ toward sinners — kindness and gentleness and forgiveness — without incurring the wrath of the overrighteous. The Pharisees of Christ's day, and of ours as well, have always looked down on the faults of others and blinded themselves to their own. And Christ would have gotten just as cool a reception today from this class as He received from the Pharisees of His own day.

Remember the time the Pharisees dragged a woman before Christ, the woman taken in adultery? They stood around, almost licking their chops in anticipation as they figured they had Him stumped for sure this time. After all, this was a very shocking sin, and they probably expected *Him* to be shocked. But over and beyond this somewhat secret wish of the Pharisees was the conviction that they were putting Him on a real spot. Here was a woman actually caught in the act of a crime which was punishable, according to Jewish law, by death by stoning. That was one law. But Christ had been preaching, and living, forgiveness. So He seemed to be in an unanswerable dilemma — either forgive her and deny the Jewish law, or let her be stoned and contradict His own teaching.

You know how masterfully Christ handled this situation, how He exposed the Pharisees for the frauds they were. He simply and quietly told them to go ahead but "Let him who is without sin cast the first stone," and then knelt and began to write in the sand. Imagine the scene: Here is a bunch of hypocrites whose only interest is in putting Him on a spot, regardless of the feelings, or even the life, of their poor victim. He calls their bluff, only stipulating that the first stone be thrown by someone who is sinless. And He began to write in the sand, probably the secret sins of those who thought they could *act* as if they were sinless.

See these proud old characters, standing around holding rocks in their hands. And see some of them slink off right away while others, putting on a show of bravado, weigh the stones in their hands speculatively, and then reluctantly drop them and move away when they begin to read the surprising and embarrassing words in the sand.

But this is only one example out of many. Christ sums up His whole doctrine of forgiveness in one magnificent parable — that of the prodigal son. Read it for yourself. Any paraphrase of a story this perfect almost inevitably ruins the story. You will recall that this character had acted the part of a teen-aged delinquent to perfection — he had insulted his father, showed him no gratitude or respect, squandered his money and disregarded his love. And yet, at the moment of this selfish sprout's repentance, not only was his father eager to forgive him, he was looking for him. But you read it. In the original, it's terrific.

So frequently when Christ meets someone who is diseased or crippled, He cures the sufferer in a remarkable way. Instead of telling him "You are cured," He will more often say "Your sins are forgiven you." Obviously He's trying to teach us a couple of important lessons — first of all, that sin is a much worse evil than even the worst physical evils, and, second, that His forgiveness comes readily at the least sign of our wanting it.

This was Christ's attitude toward forgiveness. And this was the spirit He intended should remain forever in His Church, through the sacrament of penance.

When He instituted the sacrament of penance, or confession, Christ began with a most significant phrase, "Peace be to you." And then He went on to say "Whose sins you shall forgive they are forgiven them, and whose sins you shall retain they are retained." And so He keynoted His establishment of the sacrament of penance with a phrase describing its very essence, "Peace be to you." Probably no other sacrament can instill peace to the extent that penance can, and Christ wanted to make sure that we would remember this forever.

If you look at the sacrament of penance closely enough, you'll probably see that this peace of mind has a twofold source — psychological and supernatural. Psychologically, even the mere narration of our troubles and worries and sins can help to get them off our minds, particularly when they're the kind that might thrive on darkness.

But over and beyond any psychological benefits is the spiritual effect of the sacrament — the grace that God gives us, not just automatically through the sacrament itself (although the sacrament is what *causes* the grace) but the increase of grace that depends on our own dispositions — on our humility in confessing our sins, on our sorrow and purpose of amendment and our genuine desire to do better, on our faith, and from the very fact that we are willing to put our trust in Him and His word so thoroughly.

But we've come far enough in this discussion — too far, maybe — without a definition of what we're talking about. Let's go back to the definition of this sacrament that you probably learned long ago: Penance is a sacrament instituted by Christ in the form of a judicial process for remitting the sins committed after baptism. Let's check through all the words to see if they mean any more to us now than when we first heard them.

Except perhaps for that "judicial process" bit, you should be pretty clear on the vocabulary. And "judicial process" simply means here that some judgment of the seriousness of the penitent's sins must be made so that he can be helped and forgiven.

"Remit" means to take away. So we're in business — the whole definition is clear. Now, let's go beyond the definition.

If you stop with the definition, you may end up with the wrong idea, or at least short of the right idea. Actually, there are *two* main effects of this sacrament and it's important to keep both of them in mind. All too often some people seem to think that the sole purpose of this sacrament is to take away sin. And this is often why these same people are suckers for the temptation to go to confession very infrequently. Because if the purpose of confession is only to take away mortal sin, then naturally a person should only receive this sacrament when he had mortal sin on his soul. But that is only part of the purpose of this sacrament.

Another tremendous effect is the help to *avoid* sin, a specific grace that is given directly nowhere else. The actual fact is that people who go to confession frequently are simply not the suckers for sin that others are. And the reason is that in confession they get the very special grace to avoid sin.

There are, of course, other effects of the sacrament, too — such as the peace of mind we discussed before.

But before we go any further along this line, analyzing the sacrament, and in order to benefit from all its wonderful effects, it's most important that we get a right attitude toward the sacrament, that we come to realize as perfectly as possible the almost incredible greatness of the sacrament of penance. There will naturally be a world of difference between the person who considers confession only an annoying chore and the one who looks upon it as one of the greatest *helps* God has given us. The one who regards confession as a chore will keep putting it off just when he needs it most. But the one who knows what it's all about will actually *experience* its greatness.

Also, while there are benefits which come to us automatically in this sacrament, there are numerous other advantages we gain from it according to our dispositions. If you go to confession, for instance, with a deep sense of humility you are going to gain more from it than if you walk into it stupidly proud of yourself. And, of course, you'll gain more from any sacrament, penance included, as you have more faith. Naturally, this sacrament being what it is, a little honesty isn't going to hurt any either.

But we'll have more to say about things like this when we discuss how to go to confession. For now, it is important only that we realize it is primarily a great gift rather than a gruesome job.

But let's get back to an analysis of the sacrament, so that, knowing what makes it up, we'll be better able to appreciate and use it.

Now any sacrament — or just about anything else, for that matter — is composed of matter and form. And those two words may not mean exactly what you think. (So watch it, huh?) The matter of a sacrament is, in general, the *material* connected with it (like the water in baptism), while the form is the words, or the equivalent, used in the administration of the sacrament.

To complicate things a little further, though, it must be pointed out that there are two kinds of matter in a sacrament — remote and proximate. You know that "remote" means "at a distance," and "proximate" means "close." These words mean just about that here, with a couple of technical wrinkles. When you are speaking about the sacraments, the remote matter is usually the material used, and the proximate matter is the application of that material, or *how* it is used.

In the sacrament of penance, you have to think a little more than usual to see what the remote and proximate matter are. In fact, there is even some discussion among trained theologians as to what really is the matter of the sacrament of penance.

The difficulty is that the word "matter," or "material," is used a little differently here than it is in the other sacraments. In a sacrament like baptism, for instance, theologians talk about the "matter *from* which," a sanctifying sign proceeds. But, in the sacrament of penance, they talk more about the "matter *about* which" the sacrament is concerned.

And so, theologians will usually tell you that the penitent's sins make up the remote matter of the sacrament. And they will add, further, that the *acts* of the penitent — contrition, confession, and satisfaction (or penance) — make up the proximate "quasi-matter" of the sacrament. ("Quasi," as you undoubtedly know, means "sort of.")

(It shouldn't surprise you that theologians argue about some things. You should, in fact, be glad that they do. There are, after all, a lot of things we don't know for sure, and one of the best ways of getting knowledge and certitude is through reasonable argument. And, in this case, I think you can see how there would be some hesitancy in considering that there is any relation between sin and something as holy as a sacrament. So why not discuss the question freely until we can come up with the absolutely certain answer?)

So the sins of the penitent can be called, then, the remote matter of the sacrament. Confession is, after all, concerned with sin, and would not exist were there no sin. And so, a person who has never committed *any* sin, not even a venial sin, could not receive this sacrament. Naturally, this doesn't mean you should go out and commit sins so as to receive the grace of this sacrament. Certainly there's no person on earth who has never committed at least some venial sins.

While we're talking about the remote matter, or material, of this sacrament, it becomes obvious right away that not all sins are of equal malice, and so there must be some different *kinds* of matter here. Usually, the matter of this sacrament is said to be twofold — necessary and optional. But I'd like to add a third type, even though I can't dream up a good short term for it — something which is really *not* matter of the sacrament at all, but which *should* be mentioned if you want the full benefit of the sacrament. But let's go back and explain each of these three types of matter.

The necessary matter of this sacrament is, naturally, those sins which we *must* confess. This would mean all the mortal sins we've committed since our last confession, or, as the books put it, a bit more technically, all the mortal sins committed by us since baptism and not yet directly remitted by the sacrament of penance.

(The reason for that word *directly* is that a person may have had his mortal sins forgiven by an act of perfect contrition. Or he may have forgotten a mortal sin in confession, and this sin is forgiven indirectly. And each sin has to be mentioned in confession when he gets the chance. Clear?)

Now since this sacrament is a judicial process, and since nobody can make a judgment without knowing all the facts, we have to confess our mortal sins according to species and number. We have to tell the priest *what kind* of mortal sins we've committed and how many. Often enough, people make one of two mistakes in this matter — they either go into too much detail, or they don't say enough when they mention their sins. All the priest has to hear is *what* sin was committed and how many times. It wouldn't be enough, for example, for a person to go into the confessional and say "I sometimes committed sins against the Seventh Commandment." That could mean almost anything — stealing a million dollars or a nickel; taking from a poor man, a rich man, or a church — and so on. And such things as these, for instance, make some difference in guilt. So these things — species and number — are of no little importance.

On the other hand, the priest doesn't care to be regaled

with short stories in the confessional, so the less details the penitent can get by with the better, just so the species and number are adequately taken care of. That should be enough on the necessary matter of confession.

The optional matter of confession is simply that which may or may not be mentioned, as the penitent may wish. He has no obligation, for example, of mentioning any venial sins, though he may find it a good idea to do so.

Now let's say a little about that third classification of matter I mentioned — things which are not matter for confession at all, but which should, perhaps, be mentioned. Certainly, if one of the big purposes of the confessional is peace of mind, it will help toward that purpose to confess doubtful sins.

(A doubtful sin is not one in which a person doubts about whether a thing is a sin or not and *then* goes ahead and commits it. No, that would ordinarily be a sin, unless the person involved were scrupulous. A doubtful sin is, rather, one in which a person performs a certain action innocently enough and then *afterward* begins to wonder whether he sinned or not.)

Now these doubtful sins should not be confessed as sinful, but as exactly what they are — doubtful. Nor should they be confessed from any sense of obligation to do so, because no such obligation exists. But to keep the doubt from returning to plague one, it might be advisable that these doubts be mentioned in the confessional. Then, when the temptation to stew and worry about these doubts returns, the simple answer to the temptation is that, sin or not, the doubtful action has already been confessed and any possible guilt removed.

Temptations are no more matter for confession than are doubtful sins, but they too fall under this third category of things which, perhaps, should be confessed sometimes but need not be. This may be especially true of temptations against faith and purity, because these two types of temptation have this in common — they're both the type we should run from as fast as we can. Unless you're a fool, you don't stick around to argue with temptations against faith or purity, because argument only makes them worse and increases their danger.

Both of them, too, thrive on darkness and tend to disappear when exposed to light. And so it's a real good idea to mention if you're badly bothered by either of these nuisances, because of the help and peace even their mere mention can bring. The devil would, of course, much prefer that you conceal doubtful sins and temptations until they lead you to serious worries or sins, or even to despair. And it is so simple just to say "I was severely tempted against purity," or "I had a lot of great temptations against faith," adding — if it's true, of course — "but I don't think I gave in to them."

That, far too sketchily, is the remote matter of this sacrament. Now let's spend far too little time discussing the proximate matter.

You'll recall that the proximate quasi-matter of this sacrament is the acts of the penitent — his contrition, confession, and satisfaction. Let's take them one at a time.

Now contrition is obviously sorrow. Not so obvious is the fact that it's a little more complicated than that. There are two parts to contrition, and if either one is missing it's not really contrition at all. The person going to confession naturally has to be *sorry* for his sins. But it doesn't do any good to be sorry for something if one has no purpose of amendment, and so the contrition necessary for confession has to include a sincere purpose of amendment.

Even in human relationships, sorrow without any purpose of amendment is a contradiction, a ridiculous thing. Suppose you have an acquaintance who walks up and slugs you in the mouth. Later, he tells you he's sorry for this, so you accept his apology and forgive him. Then, he hauls off and slugs you again. It gets a little harder to accept his next apology, especially if he starts to make a real habit of knocking you around. And you can't expect God to accept *your* apologies either if you have no intention of ceasing to offend Him.

Contrition, then, contains both sorrow and a purpose of amendment. And each of these must have certain qualities.

Our sorrow must naturally, in the first place, be *sincere*. That's obvious to everybody. And so is its meaning.

Secondly, our sorrow has to be *supreme*. We have to realize, at least implicitly, that sin is the greatest possible evil, greater, for example, than any merely physical evil. (Notice that this is an intellectual conviction and not necessarily a *feeling!*) That really isn't too hard to realize if we put our mind to it. After all, what could ever possibly compare with an offense against an infinite God, no matter how "slight" some would-be theologians consider such an offense!

Thirdly, our sorrow for sins has to be *supernatural*, a word that has to do with our reason for sorrow, namely, that we've offended God. It really does no good to be sorry for a sin simply because we were caught at it, or because it had some ill effect on us physically. The guy who gets drunk and is sorry for it because the next day he has a head the size and composition of a watermelon is not exactly exercising supernatural sorrow. He's only sorry because *he's* hurt, not because God is offended. The same is true of any other sin — the murderer who's sorry because he'll get hung, the thief who's sorry because he's in jail, and so forth. Not that such motives can't go with supernatural sorrow, but they're just not enough by themselves. Supernatural sorrow has to have *some* connection with faith, with God.

The final quality our sorrow has to have if it's to be valid for confession is that it must be *universal*. It has to include *all* our mortal sins and not just one or two of them. Let's go back to your acquaintances for an example that will clarify this a little.

Suppose someone has stolen $20 from you on one occasion and $100 on another. His conscience begins to bother him, however, so he tells you he's sorry for taking the twenty and that he'll give it back, but he mentions, too, that he's not sorry about the hundred, and that he intends to keep it. You wouldn't say his sorrow has very much of the universal in it. And you might find it somewhat hard to forgive him for *anything*. Now let's give God credit for being at least as sensible and reasonable as we are. He can't forgive us either unless we're sorry for all our mortal sins, even our "favorite" ones. Such "sorrow" would be a fake.

So for our sorrow to be genuine, it will have to be sincere, supreme, supernatural, and universal. This doesn't mean that every time we go to confession or make an act of contrition we have to think of all these things specifically. Not at all. But we'll know right away, automatically and implicitly, if one or more of these elements is missing. So if we don't rule out one of these characteristics or realize one is missing, we can be sure it's not missing and that our sorrow is good and valid.

There's an important point that should be mentioned here concerning the sincerity of our sorrow. All too often, our sins are repeats. We don't dig up a new set for each confession, and therefore we realize, when we go to confession, that, since we have sinned before, we are liable to sin again, even after going to Confession. And, unless we are thinking clearly and unemotionally, we're liable to think our sorrow was not sincere and work ourselves into a state of near despair.

Thinking clearly, however, we must come to realize that the sincerity of our sorrow (and of our purpose of amendment as well) has to be judged by our disposition *at the time of confession.* Even sincere sorrow can't, after all, make us impeccable. But if we really are sorry for our sins and determined, *at the time of confession,* to avoid sin, then we can be sure that both our sorrow and our purpose of amendment are sincere, no matter what may happen afterward.

And that brings up the qualities necessary for a good purpose of amendment: the very first requisite of our purpose of amendment, just as it was the first requisite of our sorrow, is that it be *sincere.* We must be determined, here and now, at the time of confession, not to sin again.

Second, our purpose of amendment, like our sorrow, has to be *universal,* that is, it must include *all* mortal sins. We must really be determined that we are going to avoid, not just the sins we find the easiest to avoid, but all sin. To invoke another somewhat farfetched example — if you resolve never to hurt a friend of yours again by hitting him with a ball bat but are still determined to shoot him in the arm or leg occasionally, this would seem to fall somewhat short of a universal purpose of amendment and would hardly cement a perfect friendship.

Finally, our purpose of amendment has to be *efficacious.* The word *efficacious* means simply that we intend it to produce its desired effect. An efficacious purpose of amendment is one which makes us determined here and now to avoid sin, not just in a vague, general way, but *to take the means* of avoiding it also. The habitual drunk who goes to confession may have sincere sorrow and a sincere purpose of amendment, but you could hardly call his resolution efficacious if he hasn't decided to take the means of avoiding drunkenness. Maybe he only and always gets drunk when he goes into a certain tavern. In that case he can keep right on resolving never to get drunk, but his resolution will do no good at all until he also decides to stay out of that tavern. Even when he gets tears in his eyes, his resolution is no good until he determines to make it efficacious.

Or suppose that a boy and girl sin together whenever they date each other. Until they decide to take the *means* of avoiding sin — double dating, avoiding being alone together, or perhaps even breaking it up — they shouldn't kid themselves that they have any real purpose of amendment. (Nor should they, for that matter, kid themselves that their sins are being forgiven. No matter how piously or how often the priest might give them absolution, they simply can't be absolved without a real purpose of amendment.)

As with the qualities required for real sorrow, so here we can be sure that the qualities required for a purpose of amendment are all present unless we make some positive act ruling out any of them. We needn't, in other words, advert specifically to these qualities. We'll know right away if one of them is missing.

These are the requisites, then, for your sorrow. Nothing new about them, but all of us need reminders from time to time.

The second act of the penitent we're going to talk about is the act of confession — the act we equate with the sacrament itself, calling it confession rather than the sacrament of penance. Confession is no more than the simple process of telling your sins to a priest, who is there in the place of God.

I said "*simple* process," and this is exactly what I meant. If your confessions become anything other than simple, something is wrong. Let's not take anything for granted here, but rather let's take a look at the normal, uncomplicated process of going to confession.

It's time, we'll suppose, for your weekly confession (which is about par for the course and not too often for anyone except the scrupulous), so you go into the church to prepare for your confession. You kneel down and remind God that you're here to brighten His whole day. Maybe you've been told that the thing to do now is check up on what sins you've committed since your last confession. But that isn't quite accurate. There's a much better way than this.

The best way to prepare for confession is to begin by realizing who's before you, that you are in the presence of God. And since this is a good way to start *any* prayer, let's give an example of a little prayer that will help you to do this:

> Oh, my God, I wish to realize that I am in Your presence and that You're now watching me. Grant, that performing this act with great devotion, I might profit from it.
>
> Oh, my God and my Lord, I adore You. I'm unworthy to appear before You. I'm sorry for all my sinfulness that's so displeasing to You. But You, my God, are infinite love and goodness, and You love me. And so I come to You, full of hope and trust in You. Give me the grace to spend this time of prayer in a way that will please You and be for the good of my soul. Enlighten my mind, touch my heart and move my will that I may know, love, and serve You ever better. Grant, my God, that all my intentions and actions may be devoted purely to the service and praise of Your divine Majesty.

So you tell God you're here and that you'd like to have His help. Then you get into what's called "the general examen" — which is not quite the same as just an examination of conscience. It has five very simple steps in it: thanksgiving, petition for enlightenment, the actual examination of conscience, sorrow, and a purpose of amendment. Let's explain each point briefly.

You begin, then, with an act of thanksgiving, which is sort of a nice touch, and which, if God *could* be surprised, would certainly do the job when all He's ever heard from you before is "gimme." You owe Him enough to thank Him — that's for sure. Among other things, you owe Him the fact that you exist and breathe and are here and able to go to confession. Maybe since your last confession you've deserved something less than this?

The second point here, the prayer for enlightenment and to know ourselves as God knows us, can be fairly brief, because we already know our sins pretty well anyhow. On the item of self-knowledge, however, we're probably not so hot, so the prayer has real meaning and importance.

In the third part of this examen, we actually examine our conscience, getting ready to confess the sins committed since our last confession. This examination, too, should be a very short process. We're aware of our sins already, and there's no use rooting around among them any more than we have to. Especially when we think we may have sinned by impurity or against faith, we should make sure we don't delay on this examination because that would be playing right into the devil's hands. He *wants* you to think back on your sins and stew about them. He *wants* you to re-think the impure thoughts that might have been sinful, because if you didn't sin by those thoughts before, you might do so now. So, examine your conscience calmly, objectively, and briefly. Then get on with it.

Being as sharp as you are, you'll undoubtedly notice that the final two parts of this examen are also the two essential parts of your contrition — sorrow and the purpose of amendment. And, in your examen, you'd probably do well to spend most of your time on these two points.

Notice, too, that if you make these two points as you should, you will have made your act of contrition before you even enter the confessional, although you are going to repeat this act while the priest absolves you. This is really a good idea, since you are a little less rushed before you go into the confessional, and you might get rattled when you're in there, or become distracted and not say it quite so thoughtfully.

That's what's known as your "general examen." It's a handy little process to keep in mind and use, not just before confession, but before you retire each night. It's actually a good, short meditation. You can do the whole thing in two or three minutes. And you may be busy, but maybe you can give God two or three minutes out of the 1440 minutes which make up each day.

(I'd like to mention here, almost by way of a footnote, another important item called "the *particular* examen." This consists in discovering your greatest weakness and then concentrating *exclusively* on that one until you've rooted it out. Or, you could do it the other way round — take some virtue you especially need to cultivate and work on it *exclusively* until you've got it. And you keep a day-to-day record on how you're doing. This is only the old principle of "divide-and conquer" applied to your spiritual life. Try it.)

So, having made your preparation you go into the confessional. And you shouldn't complicate this part of it either. Your confession should go something like this:

> "Bless me, Father, for I have sinned. (This is to give both you and the priest the gauge — a sort of throat clearer.) It's been a week since my last confession.
>
> "Since that time, I accuse myself of . . . (And here you mention your sins, taking first — if you're smart — those you're most "afraid" to mention.)
>
> "I'm sorry for these and all the sins of my past life, particularly for . . ." (And here you mention a sin of your past life that you're particularly ashamed of.)
>
> Then the priest gives you your penance and, while you're saying your act of contrition, gives you absolution. If you're not polite, you won't say "Thank you" before you leave.

Contrition and confession, then, are the first two acts of the penitent. And the last act, completing the sacrament, is satisfaction. Satisfaction is, just as the name implies, an attempt to make up for sin in some way. It comes down to doing the penance the priest assigns you — something you have an obligation to do and not to forget, but also something you don't *have* to be in any special hurry to do. There is no obligation to do or say your penance at any specific time — neither immediately, nor before the next time you go to Holy Communion, nor before your next confession. The only really important thing is that you *do* it and do not, through carelessness or anything else, omit it.

Think back, here, to something we said about that word *satisfaction*. You and I can never *satisfy* for sin. We can show our will is good, and that we're anxious to do all we can to show it, but only an infinite Being can satisfy for an infinite offense. So what? So why not unite your penance with the Mass — where you do have infinite satisfaction?

That takes care of the *matter* of this sacrament. If you'll think back, you'll remember that the form of a sacrament is the words used — or their equivalent. And so, as you might guess, the form of the sacrament of penance is the absolution of the priest, the words he uses in absolving the penitent. The only essential part of the form is very brief: "I absolve you." But, actually, the other prayers he says are really beautiful, and it's a shame we aren't more familiar with them. If you will pardon a less-than-idiomatic translation, they go something like this:

> May almighty God have mercy on you and, having forgiven your sins, lead you to eternal life. Amen.
>
> May the almighty and merciful God grant you forgiveness, absolution, and the remission of all your sins. Amen.
>
> May our Lord Jesus Christ absolve you, and I, by His authority, absolve you from every bond of excommunication, suspension, and interdict in so far as I have the power and you are in need of it. Therefore, I absolve you from your sins in the Name of the Father, and of the Son, and of the Holy Ghost, Amen.
>
> (Here he makes the sign of the cross over the person. Then he adds):
>
> May the Passion of our Lord Jesus Christ, the merits of the Blessed Virgin Mary and of all the saints, whatever good you do and whatever suffering you sustain help you to gain the remission of your sins, an increase of grace and the reward of eternal life. Amen.

That's the form of the sacrament of penance. Those are the prayers that the priest says in the darkness of the confessional.

There are a number of scattered practical points on this

sacrament which we can probably best treat by lumping them all together without much regard for logical order.

To begin with, confessions are usually heard in the confessional. This is not an absolute rule, and quite often priests will hear confessions in some rather odd places — walking around a yard, or in a hall or a room, as the occasion requires.

One of the things most often recommended for those who want to do a little more than just stay out of mortal sin is a *regular* confessor, one to whom the penitent is known, though not necessarily by name. And this is really an excellent idea, especially, perhaps, for someone who is sincerely trying to get rid of some habit of sin, or to determine his vocation, or something else which requires personal and sustained direction. This is nothing more than good sense.

Suppose, for example, a person with the habit of stealing goes to confession. The priest, in his efforts to help this penitent and cure him of this habit, gives him what he considers some practical advice. And let's suppose that the penitent finds out later that the advice doesn't work. Now if this penitent goes to confession to a different priest each time, it's easily possible that he might get exactly the same advice each time, and if it didn't work once it isn't going to work the next time either. But a regular confessor will realize that he'll have to vary his advice a little bit until he can hit on something that will work. So from this practical viewpoint, a regular confessor is important. And maybe he's even more important for the person who's trying to figure out his or her vocation in life. Of all people, this one, perhaps, needs *consistent* advice most.

It goes without saying that the scrupulous person should have a regular confessor. That's practically a "must."

A regular confessor can, then, be a real help. Another big help occasionally is what's called a "general confession." This is simply a "review" confession, reviewing as long a period of one's life as a person wishes. He may want to include all the sins of his life, particularly if he has never made a general confession before. Or, he may just want to include all the sins since his last general confession, if he makes them regularly, every year for instance. A general confession can give you a wonderful feeling, usually, of making a fresh start, and the added resolution to start serving God better. Probably the best time to make such a confession is at the time of your annual retreat — which, by the way, is another indispensable means to spiritual progress. Another good time to make a general confession would be when you change your state of life — when you are getting married or entering the religious life. A general confession then would be a tremendous help.

Incidentally, a general confession is really easy to make. You just make your regular confession, and then, when you've finished telling the sins since your last confession, you say "Since my last general confession, a year ago, I accuse myself of . . ." Naturally, there is no obligation, in a general confession to confess *any* sins, so you can leave out any you want to (which seems a little silly, no?), and you can tell your sins in much more general terms than in your regular confessions. You can, for instance, say, in a general confession, "I murdered several people each week," but in your regular confession you'd have to say "I murdered *five* people." Of course if you examine your conscience for a general confession and discover some previously *unconfessed* sin, you'll have to mention this one specifically.

Again, a precaution — the scrupulous person should not make a general confession, except on the advice of his regular confessor.

Now, what about the frequency of confession? How often should a person go? That one's impossible to answer satisfactorily in a book, because every reader is different. Certain general principles (which naturally admit of exceptions) can, however, be given. Since God instituted this sacrament as a very special help to us, we should certainly try to make use of it as frequently as reasonably possible. (This, of course, does *not* hold for the scrupulous. If you're scrupulous, follow the advice of your confessor *slavishly*. That's the way — and the only way — to overcome scruples.)

If you have committed a mortal sin, you should, of course, make an act of perfect contrition, but you should also get to confession as soon as possible. You might as well make sure you're sharing in God's life as His son or daughter, and not wasting time. And it's as silly as it is dangerous to put off going to confession when sin is on your soul. If someone were seriously injured in an accident, you'd consider him out of his head if he refused to let a doctor see him — the normal thing is to get medical help as soon as possible. It's similarly normal to want to make sure we're in the state of sanctifying grace.

I've heard that some of the Holy Fathers have gone to confession once or twice a day. Priests are supposed to go every week, as are all religious. Now, it seems incredible that the reason for this would be that priests and religious — not to mention the Holy Fathers — are greater habitual sinners than anyone else. No, the reason is more that — since the sacrament of penance is supposed to give us the grace to *avoid* sin — it's a sacrament that should be indulged in frequently. And priests and religious, whose lives are dedicated to perfection, should make use of this terrific help to perfection accordingly.

When you first examine the Church's *precept* of confession, you may tend to wonder at it a little bit, just as you do, perhaps, at the *precept* of Holy Communion. Once a year seems a foolishly rare reception of these wonderful sacraments. On further examination, though, you discover that this law isn't too bad an idea at that, both spiritually and psychologically, and we begin to give the Church a little credit for some sense. First of all, the yearly precept *is* precept, but the *desire* of Christ and His Church is that you go far beyond the precept of yearly confession and Communion.

The really big reason for this precept of yearly confession, however, is that the Church knows there *are* people who have so little grasp of what their Faith is all about that they need this sort of moral pushing around. These people go by the "principle" that if a thing isn't commanded, it shouldn't be done. Of course they don't follow this "principle" in other matters — nobody ever orders them to eat between meals or take a drink now and then, for instance.

It is possible, too, that this precept may have brought some lost souls back to Christ and His Church. The person who has been away from the sacraments for many years often feels scared and embarrassed, a state that sets up an obstacle to his return. But with this precept in mind he will often be more at ease if he feels that there are a number of people going to confession during the Easter Season who, like him, might have been away for more than a week or two.

While the sacraments were instituted by Christ as a help for human beings, He also put human beings in charge of them. And so it is that a priest — also a human being in case you don't know it — is what's called the "minister" of the sacrament of penance. He is the *only one* who can hear confessions. In days of old, just before a battle, soldiers would sometimes "confess" their sins to one another. Now this was a nice practice from the viewpoint of humility, but it was not a sacrament, and so no absolution could be given, and no sins could be remitted. Only a priest can *absolve* from sin.

Now I've heard, and so have you, quite a bit of criticism about priests in the confessional — that Father Malachy is impatient, Father Alphonsus is too strict, Father Ignatius is too easy, and that Father Boniface even refused to give some-one absolution, and so on. Sometimes the criticism is valid. (That shouldn't really surprise anyone either.) But sometimes it's unjust. Now I don't want to sound like I'm for establishing any "Be Kind To Priests Week," but I do want to say a few words about this man in the confessional.

And first of all, he *is* a man, and therefore subject to human defects — just as even you are, maybe. People expect more of a priest than they do of anyone else, that's all. And they *should* expect more. But at the same time, they should not be unreasonable in their expectations.

The priest, as such, is not just another professional man. And he doesn't mind being "inconvenienced" when necessary and when good will come of it. But don't be too rough on him when he lapses into acting human.

When a priest enters the confessional, he does not automatically shed his human nature either. He's still subject to fatigue and impatience and all other human failings. And the confessional is one of the finest places in existence for bringing out some of those failings. Some non-Catholics, you know, say that the sacraments were "invented by priests." Obviously, these people have never sat in a confessional. No priest would invent *that,* and the only reason he goes in there at all is that Christ commands it, and that tremendous good is involved.

Again, people do expect more from a priest. And rightly so. This is his job. But, again, don't hop all over him if he turns human for a moment. There are human reasons for it sometimes.

I've even heard of people leaving the Church because a priest was "rough on them" in the confessional. Maybe the priest was rough and maybe he wasn't. Maybe he had reason and maybe he didn't. But how ridiculous to leave the Church because of it! It's like a child leaving home because his father or mother — justly or unjustly — scolded him. It's saying, in effect, "I'm mad at this priest, so I'll take it out on him by going to hell."

Sometimes you hear that a priest has refused someone

absolution. (In fact, you hear about it more often than it happens!) You never hear it from the priest, of course, but sometimes a person who has been refused absolution spreads the word so far and wide that people begin to think it's a common practice. It is not. It's so extremely rare that you can say it "almost never" happens.

But "*almost* never" is not the same as "never." Every doctor loses a case now and then — often enough someone who refused to come to him until it was too late. And the priest can't bat 1000 either. There will be times when he *can't* absolve someone, when there is no real sorrow or no sincere purpose of amendment. Maybe a penitent is not willing to take the means of staying out of sin. And so the priest couldn't possibly give absolution. Even if that person fooled the priest into thinking his sorrow and purpose of amendment were genuine, the absolution couldn't possibly have any effect.

Or how could a priest even pretend to absolve someone who will not avoid a proximate occasion of sin? Let's say a certain boy and girl always, or almost always, sin together when they date. They simply can't stay out of sin in each other's company. Now suppose that the priest tells this boy that he'll at least have to avoid being alone with this girl. (This would be an attempt to break up the occasion of sin without breaking up the friendship — *if* it's a friendship at all!) And suppose that the boy refuses to make even this much effort to stay out of sin. Obviously, the priest can't absolve him. This boy is just like the drunk who says he's sorry but keeps a working flask in his pocket.

Again, let me emphasize that the refusal of absolution is *extremely* rare. After all, if a person goes to confession, there must be some motive, some sorrow, and some purpose of amendment. And no priest would refuse to give absolution unless he was morally certain that an essential disposition was completely absent.

Sometimes, people are unaware of the priest's actual attitude toward his penitents. Some of our greater modern minds seem to think that the priest sits there soaking up every word, greedily curious about what his penitents might have to say. Of course, no one in his right mind thinks like this, but the sad fact is that there are people, sometimes all too vocal, who are not in their right mind.

More frequently, perhaps, some people might think that the confessor is a hardhearted person who sits in judgment on them. They think he may "bawl them out" or treat them harshly. And 99 times out of 100, this is the furthest thing from his thoughts. (On second thought, I think we'd better make that 999,999 out of a million.) The priest's attitude in the confessional, where he comes so very close to Christ, is very much like Christ's attitude. Like Christ, he knows that his job is not to save the just, but sinners. Moreover, you would be surprised at the humility a priest feels in the confessional and the tremendous admiration he has for his penitents. And nowhere else does he come as close to sharing the feelings of Christ in His agony in the garden.

The Church wants to make sure that no single detail connected with confession should cause anyone to fear it. Probably the thing which would make some people tremble at the thought of confession would be if they were afraid their sins would be spread all over town. No such fear is possible, however, with the seal of confession in operation. The obligation upon the priest of observing this seal, of keeping absolute secrecy about confessional matter, is one of the most absolute obligations there is. And such it should be. There have been priests who have died as martyrs rather than violate the seal of confession, and every priest's attitude is the same — that he'll die rather than manifest anything heard in the confessional.

There are two types of possible violation of the seal of confession, both of which the priest is extremely careful to avoid — a direct violation and an indirect violation. A priest would violate the seal directly if he manifested the sin of a penitent together with his identity. He would violate the seal indirectly if he talked about confessional matter when there is a possibility that someone may put two and two together and come up with the identity of the penitent. No priest would say, for instance, "I was hearing confessions today, and did I hear a lot of sins of stealing!" He simply doesn't talk about it. This would constitute an indirect violation of the seal, because there's some possibility of guessing identities here.

In a sense, the priest — because of the responsibility he has, and because of psychological factors as well as God's grace — becomes a sort of spiritual schizophrenic, having one identity in the confessional and another outside it. For some reason or other, a priest simply does not refer to any confession even mentally outside the confessional. Part of it is habit, part of it God's grace, and part of it is that all confessions are pretty much alike. But, outside, his mind seems shut off completely from the confessional, as though he had never heard a confession. Most priests can face a penitent right after confession without any mental reference to the confession or even to the fact that this person has been to confession. A remarkable thing, really, but certainly not miraculous. Christ attached tremendous importance to this sacrament, so it's not surprising that His help is there to preserve its all-important secrecy.

There were two men who were very close to Christ during His life on earth, both of whom became quite prominent, each in a different way. Both of them betrayed Christ — miserably. But one had the courage and the humility to tell Christ he knew he had been wrong and to ask His forgiveness; the other turned away from Christ, to despair. Peter, who today would have the courage and humility to go to confession, became head of the Church. Judas, who would today belong with those who needlessly fear confession, turned in on himself, away from Christ.

Those are a few general ideas on the sacrament of penance. It's a tremendous gift of God, one, in fact, that only God could have come up with. If you forget all else, keep in mind that this great sacrament has *two* purposes — to forgive sin and to help you to avoid sin. You've been given an awful lot, you Catholics. So your responsibility is enormous.

Now let's look briefly at another sacrament Christ has given us, the Holy Eucharist, the special sacrament of Christ's love.

Not even the sacrament of penance can be considered as remarkable as this one, because here is Christ Himself, body and blood, soul and divinity. Try — and try often — to realize what a tremendous gift you have here. How much those who are not Catholics would give if they *could* believe in it, and most probably they would act on their belief and receive the sacrament more frequently than do many Catholics, who take too much for granted.

To make clear something I am stumblingly trying to put across — the fact that non-Catholics often seem more appreciative of things Catholic than are Catholics themselves, I would like to quote a brief article from *Time* and *The Christian Century* magazines from some time back. In this article, a non-Catholic chaplain of World War II had a few things to say about the gifts Catholics enjoy:

> In the early days of the Okinawa campaign, when our regiment was sweeping through enemy-infested territory, the Catholic chaplain and I visited one of our companies on bivouac. I roamed through the area, greeting and chatting with men. . . . The priest, however, was soon surrounded in the conspicuous center of the encampment by kneeling men "going to Confession" and receiving the "consolation of the Holy Sacrament." Something was obviously going on which was meaningful to the Catholics, and impressive to the non-churched as well as to the Catholics. I had no religious ministrations that I could

confidently use to ease the emotional tension of the Protestant wounded. The priest, on the other hand, administered the appropriate rites to all Catholic wounded. His religious rites were taken so seriously, by himself and by the Catholics around him, that he would be called out of the sack at night when the wounded were brought into sick bay.

In the early part of the campaign, when we had time to be concerned about individuals who had been killed, I was deeply distressed as we identified our dead preparatory to writing letters of condolence to the next of kin. When the Catholic chaplain found one of his men, he performed a rite that demonstrated his concern to the bystanders. He did something that satisfied their need for a token signifying their common distress. But when I found a Protestant boy, I could only gently cover his form again, while the spectators stood by in a silence heavy with disappointment.*

Sort of points up your responsibility toward the gifts God has given you, doesn't it?

The Holy Eucharist, as we learned a long, long time ago, is the sacrament of the Body and Blood of Christ under the species of bread and wine for the spiritual nourishment of souls. Undoubtedly you memorized that definition, forgot it, memorized it again, and so on. I couldn't be sure whether you're in the remembered or forgotten stage at the moment. Chances are, though, that it never got too far beyond the category of a memory lesson. Not that you don't know it and believe it, but you probably don't think and pray about it enough to make yourself *realize* it in a practical way.

How appalling it is when we first realize that Christ actually exists under the lowly appearance of bread and wine! And yet, when you think about it, these are the perfect elements for this sacrament, since they're the most common types of food and drink, and this sacrament is spiritual food, "for the spiritual nourishment of souls."

---

* From "Chaplains in Combat," by John Ruskin Clark, in *The Christian Century,* Nov. 27, 1946. Reprinted in *Time,* Dec. 9, 1946. Reprinted here by permission of *The Christian Century.*

As you read the Scripture texts concerning the Eucharist, one of the first things that strikes you is that it's really a *pledge* of salvation. Now we need all the "pledges of salvation" we can get. And Christ has told us that this sacrament will take care of it for us. "He who eats my flesh and drinks my blood," He tells us, "will have eternal life."

There are, you know, people who claim that Christ was speaking metaphorically and not literally in the Eucharist texts. There is, of course, no basis for such an assumption, and usually the argument rests on "logic" about like this: "I don't believe it literally, so He *must* have been speaking figuratively." You will remember, too, that when Christ told His listeners that they would not have eternal life unless they ate His flesh and drank His blood, He had a good chance to explain that He was only speaking figuratively. In fact, He would have been *obliged* to tell them. Remember that many of them "turned away and walked with Him no longer" because they took Him literally and wouldn't believe Him. And He just let them go — because He did mean what He said literally and not figuratively.

When you study the Blessed Sacrament, you find that there are three ways of looking at it. It can be considered as a sacrifice, as the real Presence and as a sacrament. Let's look at it first as a *sacrifice*.

We've considered the Sacrifice of the Mass already — at least in a sketchy sort of way. So let's consider just one small point here. There are some people who keep telling themselves what wonderful followers of Christ they'd be if they had actually lived in His day. They are convinced that, if He were living today, they would love and serve Him as well as any of the Apostles did, or perhaps even better for that matter. And all too often you find these same people sitting in the back pew at Mass absent-mindedly dreaming their dreams of being great apostles, and perhaps thinking of how close *they* would have been to the cross had they had the

Some people brag about how brave they would have been at Calvary, and they don't even tumble to what goes on before them at Mass.

opportunity. It doesn't seem as if they would have been very close to the cross if they can't even get close to the Mass, so much a part of the Sacrifice of Calvary. They might have gotten as far as the edge of the crowd at Calvary, but chances are they wouldn't have been even that close, because there wasn't any obligation clearly binding them to be there under pain of mortal sin. (Or maybe they would have been there at that. A bit of verse keeps running through my mind here:

> Had I lived with Christ, I asked one night,
> Would I have hung at His left or right?)

If they would spend their time doing some studying instead of dreaming, they would know that the Mass is really the re-enactment of Calvary. At Calvary and in the Mass, both Victim and Priest are the same, Christ Himself, the Mediator between God and man.

You know the purpose of the Mass perfectly well — to adore God, to tell Him we're sorry for our sins, to thank Him and ask Him for the things we need; or, as we learned in our catechism, adoration, contrition, thanksgiving, and petition. Sometimes we tell ourselves we can handle these things all by ourselves, when the only really adequate way of taking care of them is through the Mass. Go back to what was said about our inability to perform any supernatural act and about the infinite offense sin is. And you'll know that only in the Mass can we make adequate acts of adoration, contrition, and the others because here the Victim is Christ Himself.

I'm sure you've occasionally heard even very good Catholics use the expression "I have to go to Mass on Sundays." And good Catholics or not, this is probably one of the most stupid expressions ever invented. It would be a little more accurate, at least, to say "It's my privilege to be able to go to Mass."

The trouble is, undoubtedly, that our faith gets dull and our *realization* of what the Mass really is never gets vivid enough. One reason for this is that we fail to hook up the Sacrifice of the Mass and Calvary. And, second, I'm afraid that we often forget we're supposed to *work* our way to heaven — and this has to be done by faith. Don't daydream about living with Christ and then neglect Him in the Mass. And don't ever forget that the Apostles and the others who did live at the time of Christ had to have a good supply of faith, too. They had to realize that He was God even as He was being crucified. And that may have been even harder than discerning God under the species of bread and wine.

A second way of looking at the Eucharist is as the real Presence. Christ is present in the Blessed Sacrament on the

We don't have *to pass by a church every time without going in to say "Hello."*

altar of every Catholic Church in the world. If we Catholics could get a clear *realization* of this single fact, we could be well on our way to sanctity.

Practically, we should not only gain such a realization but we ought to *act* on it as well. We don't *have* to pass by a church *every* time without bothering to stop in and say

"Hello" to Christ. Nobody's going to tag you as "pious" if you do stop in, you know. As a matter of fact, you'll almost certainly have others imitating your example. And suppose someone *did* yack it up that you were going overpious? What kind of a tragedy is that? The only tragedy would be omitting such a visit to Christ because some less-than-human type might laugh at you.

In most parish churches there are special times when we can visit the Blessed Sacrament, such as at Benediction of the Blessed Sacrament. So many Catholics are actually snobbish and leave attendance at such things to those they look down on as the "pious people" of the parish. Actually, these things are intended for *them,* and there may be a rather rude awakening some day when we and these so-called "pious people of the parish" stand together — at least for a brief moment — before the throne of God.

The third way we can regard the Eucharist, and our chief concern here, is as a sacrament. Let's try to analyze it as such. Every sacrament, as we've already seen, has a certain matter and a certain form. With the Eucharist, the matter is the bread and wine and the form is the words of consecration used by the priest. The priest is, of course, the minister of the sacrament, as he takes the place of Christ, using, in fact, Christ's very words, "This is My Body" and "This is My Blood." As you know, the *species* or appearance or bread and wine remain, while the substance becomes His Body and Blood. This is what's meant by that complex word *transubstantiation*. So much for cold analysis.

The other sacraments are wonderful, but this one overshadows them all where God's love for us is concerned. The Council of Trent, which no one could ever accuse of either sentimentality or exaggeration, said that "this Sacrament must be truly said to be the source of *all* graces. . . ."

Like any other sacrament, the Eucharist gives grace of itself and it gives more grace according to the dispositions of the one receiving the sacrament. So if we receive Holy Communion absent-mindedly or thoughtlessly, we undoubtedly do receive some grace — the actual, sacramental grace as well as the grace that must come from such intimate proximity to God. But how much more grace must we receive if we're alert enough to *realize* what we're doing, and that this is actually God within us in Holy Communion, the one who loves us enough to keep us alive and to die on a cross for us — little things like that.

I suppose it's possible that there have been occasions when people received the Blessed Sacrament with the wrong motive, through pride, perhaps. It's possible. More probable, though, is the abstaining from the reception of Holy Communion because the person is afraid his motives are poor. How Satan must laugh at this sort of "reasoning." Holy Communion is what these people need most.

Another temptation Satan likes to offer is that you will become *overfamiliar* with the sacrament if you receive it too often. This is like saying we'll be overdoing it with our best friend if we visit him fifteen minutes a day. We should of course, take steps that the frequent reception of Holy Communion doesn't become mere habit. And always keep in mind that it isn't how we *feel* about a sacrament that counts. It's our conviction, our faith, and realization that count. There will be days when we will feel good about it, too, when we seem to derive great consolation and satisfaction from the reception of this sacrament. But there will be other days — and these probably will be far more frequent — when we feel nothing at all, except, perhaps, that our faith seems down close to zero. It's at times like these — when we have to really work even to make an act of faith because of the dryness God has allowed to take hold of us — that we gain most in merit and in the love of God. And if God always saw to it that we felt great consolation on receiving this sacrament, how could we prove our faith? And that, after all is what

You can't even come close to realizing the importance of receiving Christ daily in Holy Communion.

we're here for. This — as you may suspect — is not heaven just yet.

Let's be, as they say, brutally frank about the frequency of receiving Holy Communion. If I were to tell you that weekly Communion is the ideal, I'd be saying something I don't believe. Weekly Communion is a wonderful thing, true, but it really seems a minimum for the *good* Catholic. First of all, you "have to" go to Mass on Sunday anyhow. And secondly, there's really no further sacrifice involved in receiving Holy Communion on Sunday since you're there already for Mass. This is particularly true in a day when the Communion fast is so easy and simple. Weekly Communion, then, is fine. But it's hardly the ideal.

The honest fact is that there really are very few Catholics who couldn't get to Mass and receive Holy Communion every day. All the usual excuses are hurled against such a statement, of course — lack of time, getting the family off to school and work, having to get up very early if one is to get to Mass, and so on. All of these are very good excuses, as a matter of fact — or, rather, they would be good excuses for omitting something else. But not in this case. If you have even a remote idea of what the Holy Eucharist is, Christ Himself, even rather large sacrifices should be small when it comes to the daily reception of such a sacrament.

There *are* cases where it's almost impossible to get to Mass and Holy Communion on a weekday, cases where it would be very imprudent to try it. But don't automatically put yourself in this category. Ask your confessor what *he* thinks. Suppose you're still going to school. Or you work. You probably have to be at class or at work fairly early, so it would mean you'd have to get up still earlier if you went to Mass. So what's so impossible about that? You'd do it to go on a fishing trip or an all-day hike or picnic. (Maybe you could even go to bed earlier?) Some sacrifice required here? Sure. But it's hardly in proportion to the trade you're making — an hour's sleep in exchange for the privileges of being present at the Sacrifice of Calvary and of receiving Christ Himself in Holy Communion.

You know, it's always the people who have to make rather great sacrifices to get to daily Mass and Holy Communion who manage to do it. I know one prominent and very busy man, for instance, who is present at Mass every morning of the year — together with his wife and five children. I know another family in which most of the six children are still too small to corral for daily Mass, so the wife goes to Mass while her husband is home and he goes when she gets back. A man of leisure you say? Sure he is. He works a 24 hour shift at one job, and then, with about two hours in between, goes to another eight hour job, so that he works 32 hours out of every 48. And all his wife has to do is take care of six children and a home — with the usual extracurriculars. So what's *your* excuse for not receiving Christ daily?

Occasionally, a Catholic will get all fouled up about some of the requisites for receiving Holy Communion. They know, of course, that they have to be in the state of grace, free from sin. Sometimes, people — especially good people, perhaps — get confused and think they're not in the state of grace when they really are. And in case of a doubt like this, you can and should go ahead and receive Holy Communion, because such a doubt is just one of Satan's gimmicks to keep you away from Christ.

Sometimes people will come up with the blooper that you have to go to confession before every Holy Communion. It would be interesting to find out how *that* one got started. You can go to Holy Communion, without going to confession, as often as you wish, so long as you are in the state of grace. You know, of course, the tremendous benefits of frequent confession, but we're talking here about *obligation*.

Every now and then someone will get confused and figure that he can make an act of perfect contrition and go to Holy Communion if he has mortal sin on his soul. And this is wrong, too. Except in some pretty extraordinary circumstances, you must get rid of mortal sin *in confession* before going to Holy Communion.

You know, a big mystery with regard to these two sacraments — penance and the Holy Eucharist — is how utterly people fail to realize that here they have the solution to their problems. So many of us will gripe that we have great problems — moral problems, doubts about our faith, temptations of one kind or other — and it never seems to dawn on us that Christ offered us these huge helps to the solution of these very problems. You simply cannot come this close to Christ without experiencing His loving help.

Suppose that a mother and father try to figure out the best gift to get their son for Christmas. They're not wealthy by any means, so this is some problem, because they really love the little guy and want to show it through some really nice gift. Finally, they decide that it's going to be a bicycle. Now it's going to take some doing for these particular parents to buy a bicycle. But the father gives up cigarettes and the mother gives up a new hat or two, and they save in many other little ways in order to get this bike.

Come Christmas day and they put the shiny new bike that cost so much more than money before the Christmas

Sometimes we act more like spoiled kids than "children of God."

tree. And they watch eagerly to see the boy's face when he notices this gift. He does notice it, too — for about ten seconds before he loses interest and turns away to some battered old toys he's had for years. We'll suppose that, as time goes on, he does ride the bicycle occasionally to show his mother and father his heart's in the right place.

Now such a kid's either a monster or a moron, you say, and the story's too farfetched anyway. Okay — all true. But — don't we act exactly this way with regard to Holy Communion? This is God's special gift to us. And we use it only when it's not too inconvenient to do so, or when He *orders* us to do so. Or maybe we use it as a sort of "favor" to Him — to show Him our heart's in the right place! And, like the boy in the example I gave, we're either monsters or morons. But we needn't be either, if we only use our heads *and* our hearts a little bit. Try it.

persists, so that people who are bubbling over with youth and good spirits are naturally revolted by the idea of such "sanctity."

And they should be. I wouldn't say there has never been a saint who didn't have his gloomy moments because, since they're human beings, there have probably been as many types of saints as there are types of human beings. For the most part, though, the saints as a class are the least gloomy of people, because sanctity leads to happiness and joy, and only those on the road to hell have a right to be gloomy.

St. Francis of Assisi, for instance, was a man who was in love with life simply *because* he was in love with God. Anyone who can read knows that much. It's only the nonreading geniuses who know better — as usual. It was, I believe, this same Francis who came up with the expression "A saint sad is a sad saint."

Another traditional mistake of those who know history without ever bothering to read any is that the saints were a little on the "sissy" side, sort of semimanly or semiwomanly. Pick up almost any book on the saints — even one that's poorly written — and you see how stupid and unfounded such a statement is. St. Ignatius was a soldier for thirty years, and, even among that tough breed, he stood out for his courage and ability to bear suffering. When all his fellow soldiers had given up in the battle of Pamplona, it was Ignatius who stood alone on the wall and defied the enemy until a cannon ball cut him down. St. Paul traveled all over the known world in old ships, on horseback, and on foot. He was thrown into jail and beaten unmercifully. He endured almost every possible suffering for Christ and finally died for Him. Then there was St. John de Brebeuf, one of the North American martyrs. He was a giant of a man, physically and spiritually. During the incredible tortures he underwent in his martyrdom, he gave no sign that he was suffering any pain at all. So obvious was his courage that his Indian torturers actually tore out his heart and ate it, on the chance that they could gain some of that courage for themselves.

Now there are three weaklings for you! Ignatius, Paul, and de Brebeuf. Three saints. The saints were tough, sometimes physically and always spiritually and morally.

Some people get discouraged when they imagine that the saints have been such from birth. Now of course there have been many saints who were obviously given special graces even from their earliest days. There were undoubtedly many also who were innocent and holy people all their lives. But while some of the saints were of this type, there were many others who had to swerve from the road they were on to get on the road to sanctity. St. Ignatius was 30 before he swerved. Mary Magdalene and Augustine both got a late start, but both made up for lost time, too. Augustine led a life that was not just worldly but one that was almost *dedicated* to sin before he started thinking and acting straight. He mentions, in his *Confessions,* that breaking up with the woman he loved was like being torn apart. Then there was also a St. Dismas, you know, who died on a cross next to Christ and who is the patron saint of thieves. His conversion came pretty late. St. Paul was originally Saul, persecutor of Christians. There was a Margaret of Cortona who led a life of sin before turning to sanctity. There were Francis Xavier and Francis Borgia and Gabriel of Our Lady of Sorrows, who led lives characterized by worldliness before they saw clearly that sanctity was all that counted.

So don't rule out sanctity for yourself with the falsehood that the saints were born, not made. They're made — through God's grace and their own efforts.

Sometimes you can get the impression that all the saints were intellectual giants — something it would be impossible for most of us to imitate. And it is true that there were many saints with great minds — Augustine and Teresa of Avila and Thomas Aquinas, for instance. But you can't "type" the

Saints are *made, not born.*

saints this way either, because most of them were very ordinary intellectually and some were way below ordinary. The Apostles, for instance, as a group, were not intellectual giants. From goodhearted and often nonthinking Peter down to the blunt Nathaniel, the Apostles were great men, but their greatness was not intellectual. Later, there was a St. John Vianney, the Curé d'Ars, who only managed to get through his studies for the priesthood by a near miracle. And yet, his life of sacrifice, his gentle love of God and, most obvious perhaps, his heroic hours in the confessional made him one of the most personable saints of all time, although, as far as "book learning" was concerned, he was probably one of the "dumbest" saints in history. Then there was St. Joseph of Cupertino, who became the patron saint of fliers during World War II. Although he lived long before the time of airplanes, he still did a lot of flying. In fact, on one occasion the sisters in the chapel were afraid he was going to get burned up in the votive lights as he flew about the chapel. But his flying, marvelous as it was, is beside the point here. The point here is that Joseph of Cupertino gives the Curé d'Ars plenty of competition for the title of one of the "dumbest" saints in history. In fact, for a long time no monastery would accept him because he just couldn't measure up intellectually. I am not trying to advance the thesis that the saints were stupid. Where it really counted, they were the brightest of men. But it encourages a lot of us to know that they weren't geniuses on the books.

Some of the saints stayed home and "minded their own business." There were some, however, who just couldn't stay home, or maybe it was that "home" had a broader meaning for them. There were the Irish monks who used their addic-

Some of the Irish monks considered the whole world their mission-field.

tion to the wanderlust to spread Christianity all over the world. They seemed to like nothing better than to get into a rudderless boat and drift wherever Providence preferred — and as a result Christianity was spread a lot further than it otherwise would have been. There is even a patron saint of hoboes, St. Benedict Joseph Labre. So maybe there's even a chance for us bums.

An all too common illusion — or maybe excuse — is the notion that sanctity is only for priests and religious and that no one else need be concerned about it. But neither history nor logic bears this out. The Blessed Virgin was not a religious. She was married. So was St. Joseph. Mary's mother, St. Anne, was no religious. (There is, in fact, sort of a cute little prayer to St. Anne that some of you might find of interest and assistance some day: "Dear St. Anne, send me a man, as fast as you can.") St. Louis, the King of France, was a happily married man. St. Thomas More was a married man, a lawyer and a martyr in England. St. Luke, we are told, was a doctor. Margaret of Cortona was a nurse. St. Elizabeth of Hungary was married. St. Monica was the mother of Augustine. You could go on and on with this list. But that should be enough. There were saints in every walk of life and every profession, holding every kind of job. You can be a saint in any position in life. Not only that — you're supposed to be.

But if sanctity doesn't demand miracles or intellectual genius or great innocence and gifts of grace even from birth, then what does it consist in? How is it defined? It's sort of a common-sense idea to learn what it is before you pursue it. The trouble is, the only saints we read about are the canonized ones, complete with miracles. But canonization and miracles are not essential to sanctity — at least the personal, private variety of sanctity you and I are aiming at. A saint, in the first place, has to be one who *knows* a little bit about God. Then, because he does know God, he will think about Him and so come to know Him better day by day. It's utterly impossible to know God without loving Him, and, as knowledge increases, so does love.

But if we know God and love Him more each day, it follows that we're going to want to serve Him also. And this is what a saint is — one who knows God so well, he loves Him, and one who loves God so much he devotes his life to serving Him. And this service is not just for a minute now and then — it's for every minute. It's not just in great, world-shaking things but in our very ordinary actions as well. It's even thinking our next thought or drawing our next breath in the service of God.

The saints are people who try to learn all they can about God. And this they try to accomplish by every means possible — by reading, conversation, and study, for instance. They come to know that the most attractive and lovable traits they see in creatures are only the most shadowy images of God Himself, and so, through creatures, they learn about Him. They discover, along the way, that the best way of really getting to know God is through prayer. And this is why the saints were invariably men and women of prayer. But remember that prayer is defined as union with God. And this isn't a bad definition of sanctity, either — union with God.

Sanctity for us is going to consist in very tiny, practical things and not in heroics. (If we're faced with heroic challenges, with God's help we'll handle them, too.) We do not, for instance, have to imitate some of the saints in their great penances. But, while we're on the subject of penance, let's not just overlook the practice entirely. We should perform some small penances — for instance, to keep our passions and our emotions under control. Remember that your passions — such as anger and love and fear — are not to be *suppressed,* but are to be *directed* the right way, toward the love of God. The passions are good things, and you use them accordingly. But they need control, and control requires discipline. And so a little penance will help a lot.

We should also do penance to show God that our will is good, that we're willing to suffer a little out of love for Him. And as we come to know and love Christ more, we'll want to do some penance so we can share in His sufferings. This is, after all, a sign of real love — to want to share sorrow as well as joy with the one we *really* love.

If you're sincerely trying to become a saint and to do God's will, you'll recognize it when you see it. God doesn't give us orders directly but He makes use of human beings to do the job. He assigns people to direct us — superiors, teachers, parents — people like that. And they express God's will to us even when their orders may seem ridiculous. You know, we're not obliged to believe that every order we're given by our teachers, superiors, and parents is the height of wisdom. But we do have to believe that these people are in God's place, and that even if they give us a seemingly foolish order (short of sin, of course) we're doing God's will when we carry out that order. There's no such thing as a disobedient saint. The two terms are contradictory. Sanctity for you will consist in going to school when you're supposed to go to school, studying when you're supposed to study, working when it's time for work, praying when it's time to pray, and so on. So don't dream of enormous heroics when there are so many little heroic acts to help you to be a saint.

Above all, keep in mind, as you strive for sanctity — as strive you must — that, while you can't get very far along that road yourself, God and you can do *anything*.

And when you think of the saints, don't forget those two tremendous ones — Mary and Joseph. Christ's Mother — what a concept! Free of all sin — how different from us. And, perhaps above all as far as we're concerned, *our* Mother, too.

Did it ever occur to you what heroic sanctity was achieved by St. Joseph? In his life the fulfillment of every definition we've given of sanctity is perfectly obvious. He did God's will.

He obeyed superiors. He watched over Jesus and Mary with such unquestioning faithfulness and with such unselfishness that he could be said to have forgotten himself and his own wishes completely. And if ever there was selfless human love, it was Joseph's love for Mary!

Another important item on this road to God — to knowing, loving, and serving Him and becoming saints — is that we go the right way. There's a *way* for you to save your soul and to become a saint — one that is better for you than all the others. We call that way our "vocation."

Maybe you, like a lot of other people, have thought up to now that the word *vocation* applies only to priests and religious. It doesn't. So forget that little bit of narrow thinking and get the right idea.

Your vocation in life is simply the way God knows is the best way for you to save your soul and to become a saint. It's a state of life to which He directs you, but doesn't force you, by His Providence. That's your vocation, whether He wants you in the married or the priestly or religious life. What *you* have to do is think and pray and work until you find out what your vocation is, what God wants for you. And when you do find it you'll have to be generous enough to follow it, not according to your own likes, but — like St. Joseph — according to what *God* wants.

This could easily turn into a book on marriage. But there are already dozens of excellent books on this tremendous vocation — hundreds of them maybe. There isn't quite that much literature on the subject of priestly and religious vocations. Besides, you can sort of drift into marriage (though you shouldn't!) but you can't drift into the religious life.

You have to remember that the Holy Ghost doesn't come down Himself or even send an angel to tap you on the shoulder and tell you that you're supposed to get married or to be a nurse or a lawyer or a social worker or whatever you're supposed to be. So you couldn't really expect Him to use

God doesn't send an angel to bat you over the head to tell you what your vocation is.

this way of telling you if you have a religious vocation either. And yet, all too often we do expect just that.

God directs us to our vocation, religious or otherwise, by His Providence. He doesn't *force* us. This will mean that absolutely everything that happens to us or everything we encounter will have some bearing on our vocation in life. After all, as the song says, "He's got the whole world in His hands." And He has. Nothing happens without His consent. And so your entire background — your faith, your education, your parents and friends — these are all parts of God's Providence. The fact that you've heard somewhere that there's such a thing as a religious or priestly vocation — that fact is also part of God's Providence. It's part of His Providence that you were born in America and not in Russia, for instance, that you were brought up a Christian and not an atheist. It's no accident that you were taught to know and love God.

But if God *leads* us to a certain vocation, He also, by His Providence, fits us for it. Now don't get this idea jumbled up. There are very few people with only one talent. Most people could exercise their talents in any one of many states of life. You, for instance, could probably do a good job as either a dentist or a ditchdigger. And I have yet to meet a priest or a nun who couldn't have succeeded also in other vocations.

Since it is true that a person is normally *fitted* for any number of vocations there has to be a choice. He has to make up his mind, one way or the other, and choose one vocation above all the others. Now, while this is a big problem, it isn't too big to whip. There are definitely ways to determine whether we're cut out for a certain vocation or not. Let's suppose that a boy has the requisites for any number of vocations. Let's suppose also that he thinks God wants him to be a priest. He feels "called" to be a priest.

Maybe it's that word *call* that has caused some of the confusion on religious vocations, and has caused some to wait forever for some sort of clear and loud, direct call from the Holy Spirit. Actually, a vocation *is* a "call," but it's *not* a yell. God "calls" us to the religious life by very ordinary means in His Providence — by our abilities and our tendencies and such. But He does more than this — He also instills the *idea* in our minds, so that we do think about it.

Think back to the way actual grace usually works: an idea comes to our minds involuntarily, we make some judgment about it, God inspires us to choose rightly, and then we choose one way or the other. It's the same way with a vocation to the religious life — which is, after all, a *special* actual grace. God puts the idea of such a vocation in our mind, we think about it, He inspires us to choose rightly, and then we make our choice — rightly or wrongly. This is all a part of His "calling" us to the religious life. So if you've ever seriously thought of a religious vocation, you may well have one.

Now many people who could have such a vocation "reason" this way: "Everybody thinks of a religious vocation at one time or other. And not everybody can have one. So *I* haven't." You don't have to be a genius to see how illogical that one is!

And apart from its being completely illogical, one of these premises is completely wrong and the other one *may* be. Let's look.

It simply isn't true that everyone — not even everyone with the qualifications — thinks seriously of the religious life. It's amazing, in fact (until you think of how amazing God's Providence can be) to see people eminently or supereminently qualified for the religious life *to whom the thought has never seriously occurred*. And there are many such. The only answer seems to be simply that God wants them in some other life. He is not "calling" them to the religious life. So the first premise here — that everybody thinks of it — is utterly false.

The second premise — that *all* can't have vocations — is open to argument, too. I, personally, would agree with it. But there are some theologians who claim that God does offer a religious or priestly vocation to everyone, at least in some remote way. And so they'd consider the paragraph above purely bunk. Their opinion is worthy of respect and consideration, even if I don't share it. To me, the fact that some have never thought seriously of a vocation is far too striking to ignore. Equally striking is the way God almost "plagues" a person with the idea of a religious vocation when he does have one. It's not necessarily a question of thinking of it for a long period of time, either. It can come very suddenly and without warning, much as the grace that knocked St. Paul off his horse.

Or it could be a very gradual thing, an idea that has been around for months or years. It is really the seriousness of the idea that counts rather than the time element. And going with the element of seriousness is the persistence of the idea — the way it keeps coming back. It's like a yo-yo — you throw it out and it bounces right back.

Suppose, then, a boy thinks that God is calling him to the priesthood. To be reasonable about this thing (and keep in mind that you have to be honest to be reasonable), the first thing he'd do is make sure he has the *ability* to be a priest, because if he hasn't, the priesthood is obviously not his vocation.

But *ability* is a pretty big word. When you split it up a little, you see that there are three kinds of ability involved here — physical, mental, and moral. Let's take them backward and start with moral ability.

There are those who seem to think that only canonized saints or hermits need apply to religious orders.

No one — that is, no *thinking* person — has ever seriously thought that a person entering a seminary or novitiate is supposed to be a saint to start with. On the other hand, he's not supposed to have gone to pot morally either. He should be *trying* at least and succeeding, for the most part, in living an upright life. Ordinarily, neither the out-and-out saint nor the out-and-out sinner enters the religious life, though there may be an occasional exception, of course. The religious life is supposed to *lead* people toward sanctity, not just confirm them in it. So, good will and the sincere, persevering effort to lead a good life are sufficient moral foundations for a religious life.

You'd naturally expect the intellectual requirements for a teaching order to be a little more strict than those of a non-teaching order. Not that *any* order says "Only geniuses need apply." *Ordinary* ability and the willingness to work will take care of any of them. If a young man intends to become a contemplative or, as a brother, to devote his life to manual work rather than study, then naturally not so much need be demanded of him intellectually. One intellectual requirement is, of course, necessary for anyone entering any branch of the religious life — intellectual balance and common sense. No one could enter any order without these fundamental mental requirements.

There are going to be *physical* requirements, too — just as there are for any life. And these, too, are going to vary according to the type of religious life one wishes to enter. If the life is rugged, involving, say, a long course of study, then proportionately greater demands will have to be made from the health and strength standpoints. If a young man wants to become a missionary, in a very rugged foreign country, then his health will have to be rugged enough to cope with the primitive conditions of everyday life he will find there. Make sense?

So much for the "ability" required for the religious life.

Let's go on to some further requirements.

Whenever you indulge in any literature on religious vocations, you come across the word *intention*. It may seem obvious to say that you need the right intention if you're to be admitted into the religious life. Let's see if it really is so obvious.

The first thing to note is that "intention" means more than "desire." It includes motive *and* desire, both of which are of great importance in this consideration.

"Desire," first of all, means to "want something." Simple? Maybe. The trouble is that there's wanting — and wanting. You can want a thing with your will or with your emotions. And, as you might suspect, the more important type is the former. Your emotional desires can pull you the wrong way, because they're based on *feeling*. With our wills, we can desire things without anticipating much pleasure from them. We desire, for example, to be healthy and to feel good. But in order to *feel* good, there are times when we have to take some pretty disagreeable means — medicine or even surgery. And we do desire these means, revolting as they are, because we desire the end, health.

There is a parallel here with the means we sometimes have to take to save our souls, to become saints. Maybe we feel good about these things only very rarely, but we still desire them — intellectually. And the desire of a religious vocation is certainly intellectual, at least primarily. A person wants it because this is what God wants for him, but he isn't jumping up and down with glee over it. Take the boy who thinks he has a religious vocation. Emotionally, from the viewpoint of his feelings, he *wants* to follow his natural instincts. He *wants* some day to own his own home, to have a wife and children. These are good, natural desires, things men naturally want. But let's suppose he also has a vocation to the religious life, and God doesn't give him very much peace on the matter. While he naturally desires the things his nature is bent toward, he *desires* a religious vocation as a means to saving his soul and to sanctity, as the life God seems to want for him. The sacrifice of his natural desires repels him, but this is no sign that he has no desire for the religious life. He can't warp his nature, but he can know what his real desires are, despite feeling and despite the sacrifices involved. And such a person has a genuine desire for the religious life.

Personal notes injected into books can be pretty revolting, so prepare for the revolution — here comes one. When the idea of a religious vocation first occurred to the kindly old priest who is writing this book, he found the idea almost utterly revolting, and therefore threw it out. But back it bounced again and again. Finally, it just couldn't be disregarded, and it seemed quite possible he did really have a vocation. That didn't mean, however, that he'd given up on trying to get out of it. He was willing to use every natural and supernatural means to accept such a vocation, and every possible means, as well, to avoid it. Every night he said two of the most attentive "Hail Mary's" he could — one for the intention that he'd have the grace to accept a vocation, and the other that he'd be refused admission to the seminary. He was still praying that way when he hopped a train for the Jesuit novitiate. And he's been thanking God ever since.

And yet, contradictory as that former sort of thinking may have been, it's no different from the "reasoning" just about anyone goes through when confronted with a religious vocation — *knowing* what he should do and yet reluctant and even scared to do it.

But it's also true that no two vocations are alike, and there are those who look forward to a religious vocation with a lot of anticipation. They find no tremendous difficulties in accepting their vocation — only minor doubts and difficulties. And this, of course, is God's grace at work, too.

It's really amazing how vocations differ — particularly, perhaps, in the turn the desire for the life can take. One boy, for instance, will think he has to give up entirely too much to be a priest, while another will be really disturbed by the idea that he wouldn't be giving up enough. One will like the idea, while another will be thoroughly repelled by it. And yet each one could have a religious vocation. And each one has a different hurdle to overcome before he can enter on this vocation.

And that brings up the question of *motive,* which goes hand in hand with desire. Each one who enters a religious order must, of course, have some reason for so doing. And fundamental to this reason or motive must be some element of a *supernatural* motive. In other words, a person could not enter the religious life only because he couldn't get a job or was disappointed in love. Even rather silly things like these could be *occasions* leading to better motives, but they wouldn't be sufficient motives in themselves.

No, the motive for entering the religious life has to be supernatural — not supremely lofty necessarily, but supernatural. A person could, for example, realize that the religious life wouldn't be a bad way, in fact it might be a very good way, for him to save his soul. Or maybe he'd like to do something for the spiritual good of others. Another good motive. Or he might be trying to pay God back for a few things, or maybe he considers a life dedicated to God the only kind that's worthwhile. (But then, too, one can dedicate his life to God in or out of the religious or priestly life.) Or one's motive may be really lofty — the love of God. These are all good supernatural motives.

Now just because you need some supernatural motive for a religious vocation doesn't mean that natural motives are no good. They are good, and they can lead a person to supernatural motives and to the religious vocation itself. They can start a person thinking in the right direction. God, after all, uses natural means to lead us just about all the time. And there's certainly nothing wrong with looking forward to the companionship of the religious life or being attracted by the idea of teaching or by the foreign missions or even by study. These are good motives — the kind God first uses to attract us. Add some minimum supernatural motive to one or more of these (or, of course, take the supernatural motive all by itself) and you have a valid motive for entering the religious life.

A final important point to consider with regard to motive is the fact that our original motives improve and grow. The longer we're in the religious life, the more it grows on us, the more *God* grows on us. And so we soon wake up as religious to find that our motives have deepened and that whereas we began by serving ourselves, we are coming closer all the time to an exclusive service of God.

Connected with the desire and motive for the religious life is another all-important word of consideration — that of *certainty*. How certain must a person be before he's sure *enough* to enter the religious life?

Naturally, there has to be *some* certainty before one can enter upon such a life.

Obviously, he has to reach a degree of certainty going far beyond "I'll give the religious life a whirl and see if I like it." That isn't enough. On the other hand, he doesn't have to reach such absolute certainty that there will be no doubts or misgivings at all. If he's human at all, there are bound to be certain nagging little doubts in his mind — doubts about whether he'll be able to make a go of the life or not, about whether God is really calling him, about the unforeseen, mysterious difficulties he anticipates. (It's not an unknown phenomenon, you know, for people to get pretty panicky on the eve of their wedding!) These little annoyances don't ruin certainty at all. They're simply another trial God allows a person to go through to prove he's worthy of a vocation. And if he can't conquer these and put his trust in God in the face of them, he flunks the test.

To be fairly practical on this vocation idea, let's consider the biggest obstacle to accepting a vocation. Let's face it, when boys are averse to accepting a religious vocation, it's often because there are such things as girls. And you can reverse that statement, too. Sometimes a boy will think he has no vocation because he likes girls, or a girl ditto because she likes boys. But in reality the fact that they like each other has nothing to do with their possible religious vocation. Woman-haters don't become priests. If they were *genuine* woman-haters, they wouldn't be accepted for the priesthood in the first place, because the boy who really hates girls is simply not normal. (I say "genuine," because almost every boy has to go through a phase of *pretending* to be a woman-hater, sometime after that phase of his life when he figures God made girls to throw rocks at.) The "woman-hater priest" would be warped and almost useless in his job, because he would hate half the human race and misunderstand the other half. No, the boy who becomes a priest is not against the female of the species. On the contrary, he likes her enough to give up the specialized love he might some day give one woman, his wife — for a greater good and a greater love, the love of God. (And we don't "give up" the things we dislike, but only those we really like.) There's no question about it — this is no easy sacrifice for a boy to make. But then the crucifix doesn't look like any snap either, does it? (I know you'll be able to change "he" to "she" and "boy" to "girl" as required here.)

To go even further on this idea, it's possible that God might want a boy to be a priest even when he thinks he's in love, or really is in love with a girl. And, for the boy confronted with such a situation, the outcome will depend on whether he loves God or the girl more. (And don't forget that even a married man or woman has to love God above his or her spouse.)

Let's take an example of this. Here's a girl who's pretty sure she has a vocation. The summer before she's to enter the convent, however, she succeeds in falling in love with a boy. Now certainly a vocation is not a command. It's an invitation. So she can say "I'm in love with this boy. So I won't enter the convent after all." And she *may* be saying, in effect, "I intended to answer God's call to serve Him in a special way until one of His attractive creatures came along." And isn't she also saying "I'll put his love *above* the love of God for now"? Sad, but true — if she really had a religious vocation, of course.

Now, what about the person who really has a religious vocation and passes it up? It isn't exactly a command from God, so is any sin involved? Here again, there are some arguments. Some theologians say "Yes," and some — probably most — say "No." It would be extremely rash for me to try to settle a question that theologians can't settle among themselves. But I can tell you what I think and give you my reasons for so thinking.

I do not think you could say it would be a direct sin to pass up a clear vocation — except in very special circumstances. Probably, for example, a boy with a vocation to the priesthood would be bound, under pain of sin, to accept that vocation if there was a tremendous shortage of priests in his area. Or if he had a direct, personal call from the Holy Spirit and refused, that would seem fairly serious, too.

Secondly, and apart from these exceptional cases, it's hard to see how anyone refusing a *clear* vocation could avoid a certain selfishness, a lack of generosity. Just what variety of sin that might be, I'll leave to you.

Thirdly, and most important, there is the question of refusing a very special grace of God. Now we said earlier that God gives everyone the grace to be saved. We can be sure He also

Most people who put off a vocation for "a while" put it off for quite *a while.*

gives everyone the grace of sanctification. And whether it be the grace of salvation or sanctification, actual graces work in *series*. You use one grace and you get the next one; use that one and you get another, and so on. Similarly, if you refuse one actual grace you are refusing the entire series of graces that was to be built on that one. If God wants you to enter the religious life, He has a whole series of graces in store for you, to lead to your salvation and sanctification. You refuse that grace, and what happens? You have thereby refused the entire primary series of graces God had ready for your salvation and sanctification.

Does that mean you can't save your soul outside the religious life if that's your vocation? Not at all. God is still infinitely merciful. But it does mean that the *primary* series of graces God had in mind for your salvation is entirely useless, and that the next series He offers will not be as wonderful. And *that* is something to think about.

Another mistake some people make with regard to a religious vocation is to "put it off for a while," without good reason, when they are fairly certain. They put it off because it seems to them an enormous sacrifice, and they figure they'd like to spend a little more time living it up first. They're like St. Augustine who, before his conversion, prayed for purity, and always added "but not for a while yet." Of course, anyone who's completely unsure about a religious vocation should put if off until he's more certain, one way or the other. But the person who's fairly certain — with the usual doubts accompanying any vocation — is risking the loss of his vocation if he postpones it. Just because God offers you the gift of a religious vocation this year is no indication He's going to make the same offer again if you pass it up. Again, to resort to a personal reference — I've dealt with quite a number of vocations in the past ten years or so, and in that time I've seen many vocations "postponed." And never, in that time, have I seen a "postponed" vocation accepted later. That word is *never*. Granted, *my* experience is not sweeping. But the proportion *is* startling!

You see, God offers you a religious vocation at a certain stage of your life, and He expects you to accept it. Not only is there no guarantee you'll ever be offered it again if you put it off, but also, since a vocation is a very fragile thing in a sense, there are lots of "creatures" which could distract you from it — absorption in parties and dances, your natural liking for "a good time," starting to go steady, and just plain worldliness. It takes almost a miracle of grace to safeguard a vocation — and miracles of grace are pretty hard to come by.

Occasionally you encounter some rather interesting reasons why a person will pass up a vocation, or why his parents, perhaps, will say that he should pass one up. One of the best I've heard came from a father who said his boy was too smart and handsome to be a priest, a comment which drove one apparently stupid, ugly priest to the mirror. But even despite evidence like this, God simply can't want only the dumb and ugly in His special service. From the "handsome" viewpoint, certainly we don't want to give God only those left over after all the nonrepulsives have gone into other professions. And with regard to brains, this commodity has some use in God's service also. As a matter of fact, probably in

Occasionally parents, not knowing what the religious vocation is all about, will rule it out of their own ambitious thoughts for their children.

no other profession does a person develop his mind more broadly. In most professions, you develop only one special part of your mind, but as a priest, for instance, you have to develop many intellectual skills. And the more apt your mind is for this sort of development the better. "Too smart and handsome." Ugh!

Sometimes really sincere-minded boys and girls will feel that they're simply not worthy of the religious life. Now certainly God, when He established the priesthood and the religious life, knew that His priests and religious would have to be weak human beings. He knew, for instance, that there could never be anyone, outside of Christ Himself, worthy of the priesthood. So there's no use in anyone's worrying about whether he's worthy of it or not. He isn't. He couldn't possibly be. But God realizes the situation, and still calls human beings to the priesthood and religious life. That's *His* business.

Let's take up a final consideration about religious vocations. Probably whenever you've considered such a vocation, you've thought primarily of what you'd be "giving up." And this is by no means an invalid consideration. But, in the first place, we fail to notice that we're going to have to "give up" certain things no matter what state of life we get into. There is no dedicated doctor for instance, who doesn't give up a great deal of his "leisure time" for studying and for taking care of patients who refuse to get sick on schedule. And similar sacrifices have to be made in any life.

Secondly, when we give up the very little we have to offer in accepting a religious or priestly vocation, God invariably gives so much back to us that we become ashamed of the little sacrifices we made so much of. But we do have to get over the hump of what *seems* like enormous sacrifice first. Then, when God sees that we're willing to be generous with Him, He showers us with such tremendous gifts that our "generosity" looks insignificant indeed.

You know, we spend our time figuring out our vocation from every angle. We think and pray about it, and finally we decide. And — years later perhaps — we find out that all we were doing was *clearing the way* to our real vocation — that God, and not we, did the choosing. Little things, seeming accidents, in God's Providence, led us gently, or not so gently, to our vocation in life. And that's why all of us — priests, religious, or married — who are certain we are in the vocation God wants, get on our knees frequently to thank Him for overcoming our stupid objections and seeing that we went the right way. Work as if everything depended on you, but pray as if it all depended on God. That's the open secret, not just to finding your right niche in life, but to happiness itself.

But even though the preparation for your vocation in life, your thinking and praying it out, is taking place now, your entering into a state of life is in the future. A more practical question at the moment is how you can best live your *present* vocation, which is to become a saint in your own state of life. All the things we've been talking about in this book can be helpful in this regard, but I'd like to suggest one way here and now that will put all these things together for you and help you to co-ordinate your efforts. It's a way of life and a plan of life, and if you really use it, it will help to make you a saint. This is, of course, the Sodality of Our Lady.

Now hold on a minute before you close the book. It's certainly possible that you may have belonged to the Sodality at one time and given up on it because it had nothing to offer. And maybe you were never given the slightest hint that the Sodality had anything to do with sanctity. Or, maybe at best you had the impression it was a "do-good" organization, consisting *only* of external activities — like collecting money and other things for the missions — without any thought of an interior life or personal sanctity. If this is the case, then you didn't belong to the Sodality at all. You be-

The Sodality is a way of life, *permeating one's* whole *life.*

longed to something *called* a Sodality. Let's forget what we *thought* it was and look at it fairly and honestly to see what it really is.

The first thing you notice, when you study the Sodality even a little bit, is that coming absolutely first in the order of importance in it *is* the spiritual life. Don't make the mistake of thinking that "spiritual life" means just a series of devotions. Nor is the Sodality just another devotion either — like devotion to the Sacred Heart or to Our Lady of Perpetual Help, wonderful as these devotions are. It has something in common with devotions, true, but it goes beyond them. A devotion, you see, is intermittent. But the Sodality permeates your whole life without interruption. You are a Sodalist, not just on First Fridays or First Saturdays, but all day long, every day. The Sodality is, to put it most briefly, *a way of life,* or a way of living your life, no matter what your state of life and no matter what other devotions you practice along with it.

Since the Sodality *is* a way of life, it must have some very definite purpose. In general, of course, its purpose would have to be to make us better Catholics. But this is true of any devotion as well. And so the first purpose of the Sodality goes beyond this and has as its objective the formation of

Catholics, Catholics who are *consistently* aiming at something higher than the duty-and-nothing-more existence. The Sodality helps to produce exemplary, outstanding Catholics, those who are good Catholics and proud of it and who are willing to show the world what a genuine Catholic is like. In other words, the Sodality tries to — and does — produce Catholics who are not afraid to act as they should publicly as well as privately.

That's part of its purpose. And if the purpose of the Sodality is to produce exemplary Catholics, then its primary purpose must be the salvation of the souls of its members. And since the word *exemplary* is used, then the Sodality's purpose must also include the betterment or perfection of souls as well. That's a good start, then, on what the Sodality is for — the salvation and perfection of one's soul.

But the Sodality, being the kind of organization it is, will go beyond this, turning to the salvation and perfection of the souls of others as well as the souls of its members. And

The first thing you notice about the Sodality is that it has to do with the spiritual *life.*

so the element of apostolic work enters into the scope of the Sodality, too, and we can now state its complete purpose as "the salvation and perfection of one's own soul and the salvation and perfection of the soul of one's neighbor."

When you're told the purpose of something, it's also nice to be told a little something about the means of accomplishing that purpose. In the Sodality, the means are easily described: "To Jesus through Mary." This organization is known as the Sodality *of Our Lady,* and it means exactly that. The very word *Sodality* means companionship; and Sodalists are to be companions, not just of one another, but primarily of Mary.

Devotion to Mary is the fundamental characteristic of a Sodalist. What are some of the other requisites? A Sodalist should be willing proudly to defend his Faith — literally, and not just figuratively — whenever this is called for.

Occasionally people come up with the mistaken idea that only priests and religious are supposed to work toward perfection (or sanctity) or to help their neighbor to save his soul. Actually, this is everyone's job no matter what his state of life. And a fireman or a policeman or a priest or a dentist or anyone else can be a good Sodalist, sincerely trying to sanctify himself in his state of life and trying to help others to do the same for others in *their* state.

But the Sodality is not just a group of *individuals,* either. It is individuals organized and working together for a common goal. Sometimes it's pretty tough to do the things we know are right if we have to do them alone. But when we have some company, when our companions are all working with us toward a common goal, things get a lot easier.

This "solidarity" of the Sodality is going to vary quite a bit according to circumstances. In some schools, it will be more apparent than in others, just as your Sodalities in some schools will be better than in others. Sometimes your parish Sodality will really be unified. At other times you'll almost have to go it alone as a Sodalist.

It's a lot easier to do what's right when we know we have company in doing it.

Ideally, though, and very often in fact, the Sodality is an organization, and Sodalists work together toward their common goal. This is one big reason for such things as city and state Sodality unions, for Sodality conventions and publications and the like — to exchange ideas and to profit by example.

Another feature of the Sodality that contributes to its solidarity is the great number of privileges that go with membership. A Sodalist, for example, can receive any number of plenary indulgences, if he's on the lookout for them. He can receive a plenary indulgence at the time of his reception into the Sodality, at the hour of death, on the feasts of our Lord and of our Blessed Mother by going to Mass and receiving Holy Communion, and on World Sodality Day. It may surprise you to know that any Sodalist can receive a plenary indulgence by attending the weekly Sodality meeting and going to Mass and Holy Communion and confession within a week either way and saying a few prayers for the intention of the Holy Father. He can also receive a plenary indulgence at the time of his annual retreat and at Sodality days of recollection. A Sodalist who is sick can receive a plenary indulgence when visited by the director of the Sodality. And there are a lot of other indulgences, both plenary and partial, which can be gained by members of the Sodality.

But if a Sodalist has privileges, he must also have duties. To see what some of these are, let's look at the Sodality's structure.

The Sodality goes back to the sixteenth century shortly after the time of St. Ignatius, when it was founded by a young Jesuit. In fact, the beginning of the Sodality is almost contemporary with the beginning of the Society of Jesus. The

The Sodality is an organization, *and Sodalists work together toward their common goal.*

Society of Jesus was approved in 1540 and the Sodality was approved in 1563.

At any rate, this young Jesuit, Father John Leunis, noticed that among the boys he taught were many who wanted to aim at a little more than others spiritually. He recalled that he himself was following a good blueprint to sanctity in his Jesuit rules, and it occurred to him that his boys might profit from these same rules. So he wrote an adaptation of the Society's rules for these boys. The organization which came into being and was to follow these rules came to be known as the Sodality of Our Lady.

And right away, a somewhat common misconception can be cleared up. Somewhere along the line, someone got the brilliant idea that the Sodality is an organization for women only. (This probably began, as most calumnies do, as a defense mechanism, made up by someone who didn't have the courage to live up to the Sodality way of life himself.) The original Sodalities were founded for boys, and it was many a year before any girls at all were admitted. Today, there are great numbers of girls in the Sodality, but there are plenty of boys also. You get a little burned at times when you hear some infallible type pronouncing that the Sodality is only for women when it is so obvious that he knows nothing about it, either by knowledge or experience.

I mentioned that the Sodality rules are an adaptation of the Jesuit rule of life. The first thing you notice about these rules, of course, is that they inculcate *striving for* holiness. Most of those who join the Sodality are not saints to begin with, but they do have the *desire* to become exemplary Catholics and saints. And they expect to get plenty of help in becoming saints from the Sodality.

Now certainly one can become a saint outside of the Sodality, and many have done so. But the Sodality is a big help to sanctity, largely because of the means and helps it embodies. You couldn't live the Sodality way of life with any degree of faithfulness and not come closer to sanctity. There is, for example, Rule 34 which treats of a Sodalist's spiritual exercises. A Sodalist is to attend Mass and receive Holy Communion frequently, daily if possible. He's to examine his conscience every evening and make an act of contrition. He's to say three Hail Mary's, and the acts of faith, hope, and contrition each morning. The rule mentions that the Sodalist should dedicate every day to God through the "Morning Offering."

This rule also states that a Sodalist should perform fifteen minutes of mental prayer every day. Now meditation or mental prayer, as you may know, is not the easiest thing in the world, and yet it's not terribly difficult after you've worked on it a little bit. You've learned something about it, I hope, from a previous chapter of this book. One practical suggestion that could be made here is that you might try making this fifteen minutes of mental prayer right after Holy Communion, as a part of your thanksgiving. You can think of who's with you, why He's with you, what He can do for you and how He loves you, and you can realize what a miraculous, marvelous thing this is, that God, who has already lowered Himself enough to become man, lowers Himself much further here, under the appearance of bread and wine.

So you see that even this Rule 34 all by itself can be a tremendous help to sanctity. There are others. There are, for instance supposed to be corporate Communion days for Sodalists once a month or oftener. Frequent days of recollection are suggested. Sodalists are supposed to make a retreat every year. Along this line, I suppose most of you probably make a yearly retreat at school, but maybe sometime you could get a group of Sodalists together and make a *Sodality* retreat, one slanted toward Sodalists and not just toward those who "would like" to stay out of sin when it happens to be fairly convenient. Such a retreat could stress sanctity as well as salvation.

But there's more to the Sodality than prayer, too, because this is a practical, and not just a theoretical organization. The rules suppose that a Sodalist also keep himself away from the occasions of sin and from worldliness. And so, there are certain things in which a Sodalist has to differ from the ordinary "worldling." The Sodalist, for example, must have a deeper, more reasonable attitude toward purity than the person who is making only a halfhearted attempt to stay out of sin. The Sodalist concentrates more on the positive virtue of purity. He is more careful about the *outposts* which guard purity. Probably many people who skirt the edges of impurity do so simply because they're blindly following the crowd. But a Sodalist is trained to lead the crowd, or to follow the crowd only when it goes in the right direction.

A Sodalist should bring this attitude to every detail of his life. He should be a little more careful of his reading, of the plays and movies he goes to, of anything in fact, which might tend to give him a worldly or careless attitude. Naturally, every good Christian has to be careful of these things, but a Sodalist should be more careful than the others because he's aiming higher.

Come to think of it, "careful" is not the best word here. What I really mean is that a Sodalist should be more concerned with getting closer to God than in soaking up a little more worldliness. And if he's going to get anywhere along that line, there's another virtue a Sodalist has to have — freedom from human respect. The Sodalist, of all people, must never be deterred from a course of action simply because he thinks someone might laugh at him. The question he asks is not "What will others think of this?" but rather "Is this going to get me closer to God or isn't it?" You girls are certainly familiar with the type of little girl who figures — usually aloud — that she has to do everything a boy wants, has to allow him any liberty whatsoever on a date because otherwise he might think she's a square and might not ask for another date. But the girl who lives as a Sodalist has more sense as well as more principles. (Of course, the joker in this particular deck is that the girl who looks for popularity through sex is liable to end up more neurotic than popular.)

Another way of putting this would be to say that the Sodalist should be more spiritually independent than others. He doesn't beat others over the head with his spirituality but calmly goes his own good way. The Sodalist who hears another boy — or girl — boasting about what an impure pig he was the night before can act like a Sodalist by matter-of-factly showing that he doesn't want any part of the conversation and by showing that such things are beneath him, not just as a Sodalist, but as a rational, mature human being. The Sodalist will realize that it's only the immature, stupid fake who thinks that impurity and drunkenness, for instance, are things to be boasted about.

Much more than this could be said about a Sodalist's *personal* sanctification — *if* this were two books instead of one. Think about these things. Pray about them. But, here and now, let's say a word about that second purpose of the Sodality — the salvation and perfection of your neighbor.

And let's begin with a reminder. You don't make sure, first of all, of your own salvation and perfection and only then go on to work on the salvation and perfection of others. No, you do both jobs at once.

You see, when you perform apostolic works you not only help others but you help yourself as well. Part of this effect is natural and psychological, because you may *feel* good when you help others. But a greater part of it is supernatural and comes from the grace of God. You perform apostolic works because you possess the inner spirit of the Sodality. And in performing these apostolic works you increase that spirit — by God's grace.

But just what can a Sodalist do by way of apostolic work? Certainly the first form of such activity, its essential mani-

Sodalists carry out a lot of apostolic projects together.

festation, is the Sodalist's own good example. That's easy enough to see. But we have to be careful that we don't simply equate example and apostolic work and let it go at that. That could be just an excuse for not doing anything else.

Charity is supposed to begin at home, and so is a Sodalist's apostolic activity. And so, if he's interested in helping toward the salvation and perfection of others, he ought to begin with his fellow Sodalists and do all he can for them — by his example and every other means possible.

Sometimes there will be Sodalists who seem to think that there are no good apostolic projects. (And, invariably, such an opinion could only be formed by one who is just not looking!) But the truth is that there is so much work waiting for Sodalists to do that they'll never even be able to scratch the surface. I suppose, for instance, that most Sodalities collect food baskets for the poor at Christmas time, a wonderful apostolic project. But how much do most Sodalities do for the poor outside of the Christmas season? There are hundreds of orphans in any city who would be thrilled and helped immeasurably by being given some attention — being brought to dinner and to a show sometime, for instance — during an ordinary humdrum week. There are the sick poor to be visited in and out of hospitals. There are countless children who need to be instructed in their catechism. There are innumerable apostolic projects around your school alone — a modest dress campaign, or a clean language campaign, for instance. Your school Sodality can start a "perpetual Rosary" campaign with the Sodalists reciting the Rosary in pairs, say, throughout the lunch hour. You can start a campaign to get

Sodalists can do a lot of good with a food-drive for the poor at Christmas.

people using the missal at Mass, or to get everyone to carry a rosary and use it every day, or to encourage visits to the Blessed Sacrament. There can be such things as class Communion days, or days of recollection — for your class or your Sodality or your school, or even for all the Sodalists of a city. A city-wide Sodality rally, if well planned can be a real apostolic activity. Panels on "the Sodality spirit" or other timely subjects can have a terrific impact. Sometimes, in fact, they also make a good TV show. There are, in fact, so many Sodality projects possible that you can't possibly list all of them.

The Sodality can help you to acquire certain distinctive virtues. The boy or girl, for instance, who really lives up to the Sodality way of life will probably become more of a leader than one who couldn't persevere in that life. The faithful Sodalist should become a person of great kindness and thoughtfulness, because a sincere Sodalist could hardly be an essentially selfish person. The terms — *Sodalist* and *selfishness* — are contradictory. And this unselfishness will come in everywhere for the Sodalist — at home, toward his parents, on dates, toward his companions, and especially, of course, in his spiritual life, toward God. The Sodalist is supposed to imitate Christ in the most perfect Sacrifice of all times, that of the Cross. And he strives to make these unselfish sacrifices, not for praise or for self-glorification or recognition of any sort, but for the love of Christ. As the Sodalist gets more and more of the true Sodality spirit, he will try to do his apostolic work anonymously, seeking no credit from anyone on earth but waiting for all his "credit" until the day he meets the Leader of his Sodality in heaven.

As with everything else in your school days, your school Sodality — college or high school — is a *training* Sodality, so that in the course of your schooling you should gradually learn the perfect Sodality way of life. Then, by the time you get out of school, into the parish and on your own, you will be capable of acting as perfect Sodalists without prodding or coddling. You should go from school into your vocation, not just as an expert in that vocation, but as an expert Sodalist as well. You should, in other words, bring Christ with you into your profession and state of life. You should be a Catholic in action as well as in name, able and willing to profess your faith with matter-of-fact courage.

All this the Sodality can do for you — if you give it a chance. It is one very efficient and very practical way of making sure you're on the road to sanctity. There are other ways, too. Use any and all means to get there — where you belong.

EPILOGUE

Here and there, throughout this book and the previous two books of this series, there has been quite a bit said about your only purpose in life — salvation and sanctity — and about the means of attaining that purpose. There have also been a few stumbling attempts made, in these pages, to *define* sanctity. Ultimately, you can define sanctity in only one way: Sanctity is the love of God.

Now I could spend a lot of time here, at the end of this book, talking about the love of God. It will be better, though, if *you* think and pray about it yourself, with only a few suggestions to guide you. I know no better summary of the things we should know about the love of God than that contained in the *Spiritual Exercises* of St. Ignatius, a little book you must pick up and look at sometime. This part is called "The Contemplation for Obtaining Love." Read it. Study it. Pray about it. It's in the form of a meditation, and it goes like this:

CONTEMPLATION FOR OBTAINING LOVE

Two things are to be noticed here:

The first is, that love ought to be found in deeds rather than words.

The second is, that love consists in mutual interchange on either side, that is to say, in the lover giving and communicating with the beloved what he has or can give, and on the other hand, in the beloved sharing with the lover, so that if the one have knowledge, honor, riches, he share it with him who has them not, and thus one shares all with the other.

The usual preparatory prayer.

The first prelude is a composition of place, and it is here to see myself standing before God our Lord and His angels and saints who are interceding for me.

The second prelude is to ask for what I want. It will be here to ask for an interior knowledge of the many and great benefits I have received, that, thoroughly grateful, I may in all things love and serve His Divine Majesty.

The first point is to call to mind the benefits received, of my creation, redemption, and particular gifts, dwelling with great affection on how much God our Lord has done for me, and how much He has given me of that which He has; and consequently, how much He desires to give me Himself insofar as He can according to His Divine ordinance; and then to reflect in myself what I, on my side, with great reason and justice, ought to offer and give to His Divine Majesty, that is to say, all things that are mine, and myself with them, saying, as one who makes an offering, with great affection:

"Take, O Lord, and receive all my liberty, my memory, my understanding, and all my will, whatsoever I have and possess. Thou hast given all these things to me; to Thee, O Lord, I restore them: all are Thine, dispose of them according to Thy will. Give me only Thy love and Thy grace, for this is enough for me."

The second point is to consider how God dwells in creatures, in the elements giving them being, in the plants giving them growth, in animals giving them feeling, and in men giving them understanding, and so in me giving me being, life, feeling, and causing me to understand; making likewise of me a temple, since I am created to the likeness and image of His Divine Majesty; and then reflecting on myself in the same way as has been said in the first point, or in any other way that I shall feel to be better. And let the same be done in regard to each of the following points.

The third point is to consider how God works and labors for me in all created things on the face of the earth, that is, *habet se ad modum laborantis* (behaves like one who labors), as in the heavens, elements, plants, fruit, cattle, and so forth, giving them being, preserving them, giving them growth and feeling, and so forth, and then to reflect on myself.

The fourth point is to see how all good things and all gifts descend from above, as my limited power, from the Supreme

Lili fell in love with the puppets, but she didn't have much use for their master.

and Infinite Might on high, and in the same way, justice, goodness, pity, mercy, and so forth, just as the rays descend from the sun, and waters from the spring. Then to conclude by reflecting on myself, as has been said before.

To finish with a colloquy and *Pater Noster*.

Maybe this particular summary will appeal to you and

maybe it won't. But some such scheme should be used, and regularly, to keep the love of God fresh in your mind and heart.

Maybe you were lucky enough to have seen a wonderful movie called *Lili*. Lili was a little French girl, young and cute and — in the right sense — simple. She was an orphan who had come to the big city to find her uncle. But the uncle was gone, and she fell in with a carnival group. Now Lili was an affectionate girl and she was lonely. And so it was that she fell in love — not with a man, but with a group of puppets. Whenever she could, she would watch the puppet show, during the regular performances and even when the man running the show was practicing — sometimes, unknown to her, just for her benefit. But the puppet master always seemed a surly sort of character to Lili, and so, while she came to love the puppets, she seemed to hate their master.

In each puppet she came to notice and love a different characteristic — in one a sense of humor, in another a sort of lovable grouchiness, in still another an affectionate nature, and in all three a great love and devotion to her.

Came a day when Lili grew up, when it dawned on her that all the qualities she saw in the puppets actually had their source in the puppet master. And, so, growing up, and seeing behind the puppets to their master, she saw that she really loved him, because she had seen little shadowy manifestations of his goodness and lovableness in his puppets. She had made the same mistake we all make — failing to see that all the beautiful and lovable and wonderful things we see in creatures had to be put there by God, who is infinitely wonderful. We fall in love with one quality in this creature and another quality in that creature, and all the time, until we grow up, until we become mature and wise enough, we love only creatures, blind to the beautiful God who made them. Let's ask God that we come to know Him well enough to love Him, and love Him enough to dedicate our lives to serving Him.

And let's never forget those few all-important words of St. Ignatius: "The first is, that love ought to be found in deeds rather than words."